I0881522

BOOST YOUR CREATIVITY

TO START IS TO BEGIN

CREATIVITY ISN'T A LUXURY

It's not something for later in life, when things begin to calm down. It's how we connect. How we adapt. How we find meaning, even in chaos.

This book is here to help you remember that part of who you are – and to give it room to stretch.
I didn't write this because I always feel creative.
I wrote it because often I don't. I'm a creative who suffers from imposter syndrome.
Every new project comes with a quiet voice saying,
"This time, they'll see you've got nothing."
I'm a chronic overthinker, a master procrastinator, and I've spent far too much time hesitating.

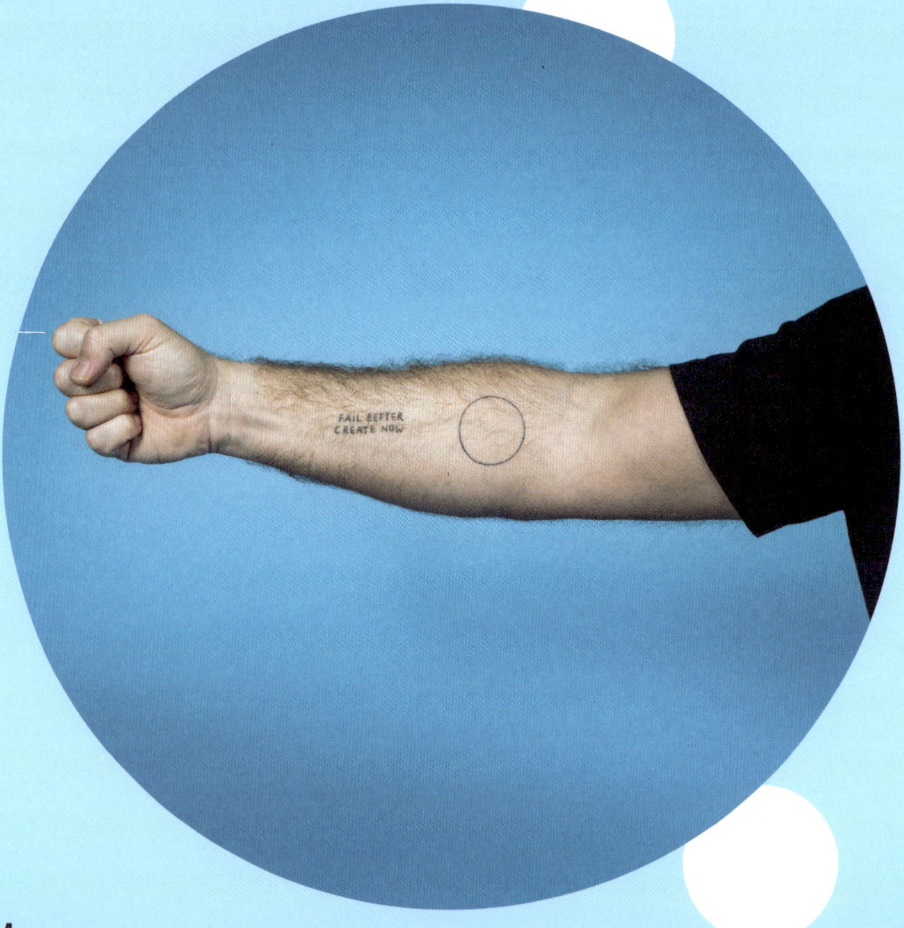

So I made a choice: I got inked.

On my left arm (in Dutch): **DON'T HESITATE, DO IT.**
On my right: **FAIL BETTER, CREATE NOW.**

It's my reminder to myself that action creates action.
Like **Robert Frost** who said:

"The best way out is always through."
(*A Servant to Servants*)

So perhaps the only way out of doubt is through action? And more is more – and every messy start holds the seed of something real.

This book is for you – and for me. For anyone who wants to remember what they're capable of, and surprise themselves along the way.

LET'S BEGIN.

Create an environment where you are free to express what you're afraid to express.

Rick Rubin—American record producer

FIND YOUR SPACE

Before you dive in, take a moment to find your space.

Not a perfect space. Not a quiet cabin in the woods or a sunlit studio with soft jazz playing in the background – unless you have one, in which case, great.

But for everyone else: your space might be messier. It might be your desk at home, surrounded by lots of to-do lists, a seat on a bus. A table in a loud bar, the bed in your dorm or the waiting room at your dentist's office. It might even be five quiet minutes in your car, parked somewhere you shouldn't.

It doesn't matter where you are.
It matters that you show up.

This book is your space to explore. To play. To wonder. To get it wrong. To be weird. To get honest. You don't need the 'right' mindset. You don't need a plan.

All you need is to be here – fully, gently, just as you are.

You don't need to build this space. Because it's something you allow. So let this book become a doorway into that space – wherever and whatever it may look like.

Welcome in.

CLAIM YOUR SPACE

Take a moment to arrive.
This is your space.
Your time.
Your permission to explore.
You don't need to explain.
Just answer the questions.

1 Where are you right now?

(Describe the space, the sounds, or the vibe in one sentence or a few words.)

2 Why did you open this book today?

(A reason, a mood, a word. No wrong answers.)

3 One quiet wish for this journey:

(For yourself, your creativity, your process.)

Creativity is not a talent. It's a way of operating.

John Cleese—English comedian

DRAW YOURSELF WITH YOUR EYES CLOSED

That's it. You're in.

THIS IS ME TRYING TO LOOK AS TOUGH AS A CREATIVE CAN BE BUT LOOK CLOSELY AND YOU'LL SEE THE SPELLING MISTAKE. #FAIL

WE'VE BEEN SOLD A LIE

They tell us creativity is a talent, something you're either born with or not.
But here's the truth: creativity is not a talent.

It's a way of being in the world.

It's not about being the best artist in the room.

It's about staying curious.
It's about noticing what others miss.
It's about experimenting, playing, asking,
"What happens if I try it like this?".

Creativity is in how you make your morning coffee.
What you are wearing today.

How you solve a problem. How you rearrange your desk, your ideas, or your thinking.

You don't have to be 'gifted'.
You just have to show up and keep an open mind.

When you operate this way, when you have a creative mindset, you don't wait for the perfect idea.

You explore all ideas. You don't fear mistakes, you respect them, and you don't seek certainty, but you follow your curiosity.

This book isn't about helping you 'become' creative.
It's about helping you remember that you already are.

You can't use up creativity.

The more you use, the more you have.

Maya Angelou—American writer

START TRAINING

Creativity isn't magic.

It's a muscle.

And like any muscle, the more you use it,
the stronger it gets.

The problem? Most of us stop using it.

Somewhere between childhood curiosity and adult responsibility, we're told to colour inside the lines, do things the 'right' way, and not be weird.

Our creativity muscle shrinks – not because we're not creative, but because we stopped flexing it.

But here's the good news: muscle memory exists.

And creativity comes back faster than you think.

Every time you write down a wild idea without editing it, doodle just for fun, or ask **"What if?"** instead of **"What is?"**, you're training that muscle.

Every small act – no matter how silly, quick, or strange – counts as a rep.

Some reps will feel awkward.

Some days you'll draw a blank.

But keep going.

You're building something.

This book is your creative gym.

The more exercises you do, the easier it becomes to lift heavier ideas, jump into new projects, and stretch into wild new directions.

So don't wait for inspiration. Train for it.

If you don't know where you are going, all roads lead there.

Lewis Carroll—English author

THINK LIKE A TRAVELLER

The journey changes you.

When you're travelling – truly travelling – everything feels different.

The streets, the smells, the sounds.
The way people greet each other.
The colour of the sky.
Even your own reflection in the mirror can seem familiar and strange at the same time.

What makes travelling such a powerful catalyst for creativity isn't just the newness.

It's the shift in perspective.

As a traveller, you're always noticing, always questioning. You ask yourself questions like **"Why do they do it this way?"** or **"What does this mean here?"** and **"How does this connect to what I know?"**.

You're curious.
You're open.
You're ready to be surprised.
You take a corner without knowing where it leads.
You get lost just so you can discover new places.

Now imagine if you could bring that same mindset to your daily life.

What if you looked at your routine as if you'd never seen it before?
What if you tried something as though it were completely new?
What if you let yourself feel lost, just so you could discover?

Thinking like a traveller isn't about physically going somewhere else. It's about taking a fresh look at what's right in front of you. It's about exploring ideas, experiences, and perspectives as if you've just arrived and everything is waiting to be discovered.

Curiosity is the quiet spark behind every breakthrough.

It's what makes you tilt your head when you look at a cloud to better see the shape. And makes you wonder what's behind that closed door.

It's the voice that asks, **"What if?"**, **"Why not?"**.

Creative people aren't always the most talented – they're often just the most interested.

They notice things.
They pay attention.
They follow the breadcrumbs.
They ask better questions.

Being curious doesn't mean having all the answers.
It means staying open to being surprised.
It means exploring without needing a result.
So don't be afraid to ask weird questions.
Investigate small moments. Zoom in on what others skip.

Curiosity is your compass.

Let it guide you. Use it.

When you think like a curious traveller, every creative problem becomes an adventure.

Every blank page is a new map.
Every question is an opening to new opportunities.

And the best part is, the journey never ends.

THE WHY BEFORE THE WHAT

Sometimes, before I begin to work on something – a project, a film, even this book – I stop and ask:

"Why am I doing this?"
Not in a dramatic, soul-searching kind of way.
Just ... out of curiosity.

It's easy to jump into the what – write a thing, make a thing, fix a thing. But when I skip the why, I often lose the plot midway.

The spark fades. The thing feels empty.
And I'm left wondering why I started at all.

The author and inspirational speaker **Simon Sinek** famously puts the WHY at the centre of everything. His *Golden Circle* helps people reconnect with purpose:

Why – How – What.

But I was raised with a different approach to this theory.

Jef Brouwers, a psychologist and also my father, draws it differently. He places the WHY on the outside of the circle – as something to return to, again and again, as you work your way inward. Because even though most of us say we care about the why, we usually begin with the what. Starting with the why helps you slow down and delve deeper.

It grounds you in meaning before movement. It's not about having all the answers – it's about remembering what drew you here in the first place.

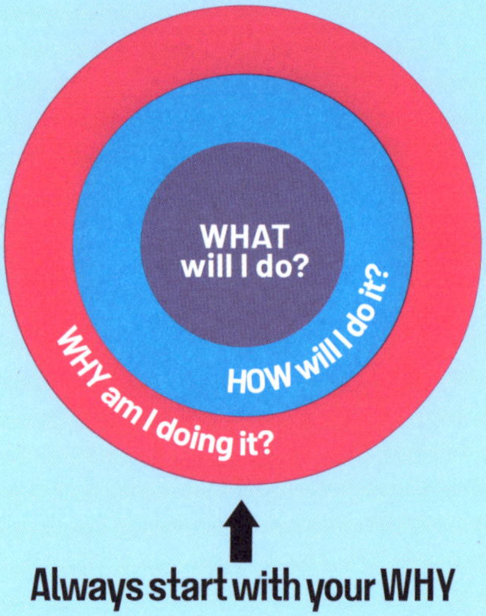

So try this: as you open this book, or flip to a new page, stop and ask yourself:

Why this one?
Why now?
Why does this idea draw me in?
Why might it unlock something I didn't know I needed?

You don't have to explain it.

Just feel it.
Let it sit with you.

When you begin with a sense of why, something shifts.

You write with more intention.
You play with more permission.
You move from impulse to purpose – not to be perfect, but to be present.

You don't need to know where this is going. But it helps to know what made you start in the first place.

Let that be enough.

Take a look at this maze.

FIND YOUR WAY FROM RED TO BLUE

Now turn the page.

DID YOU TAKE THIS PATH?

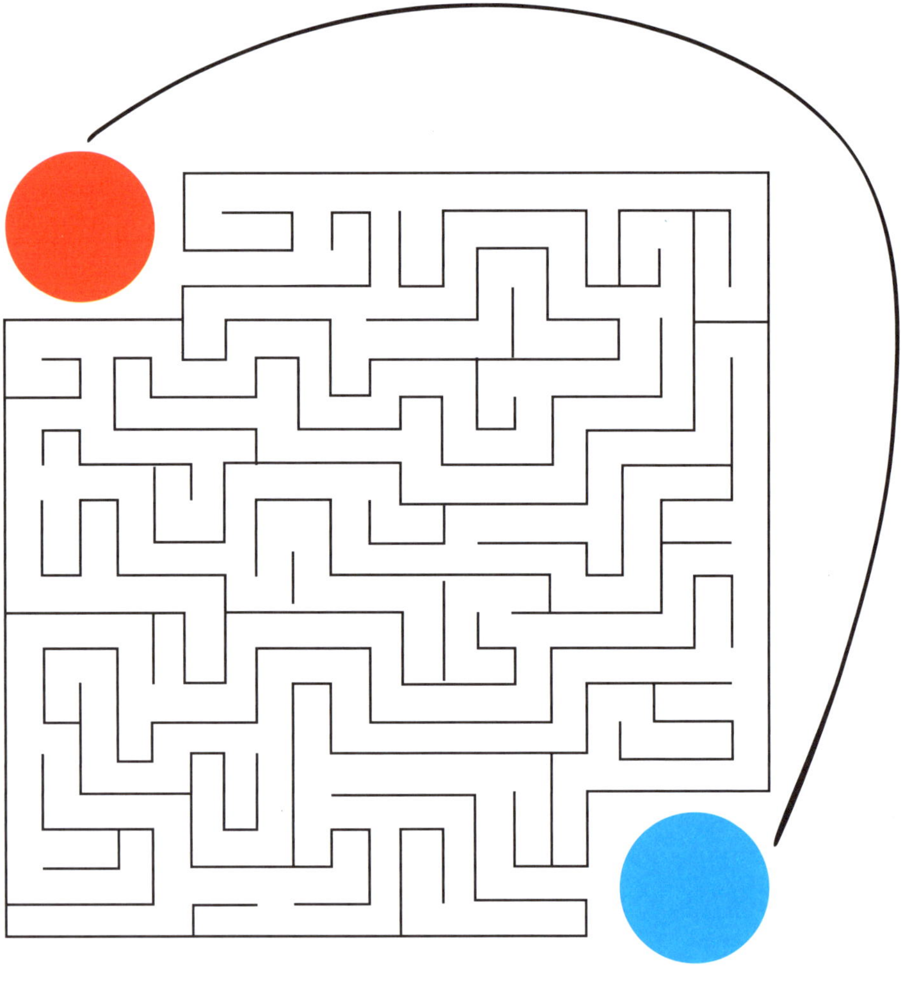

LOOK SIDEWAYS

Reframe the question, shift your perspective – this is where creative breakthroughs often happen. Instead of approaching problems or ideas head-on, imagine stepping off the path.

What happens when you go for a different angle? When you take the scenic route through your imagination instead of the highway of assumptions?

This mindset – of detours, zooming out, flipping things over – is beautifully captured in **Alan Fletcher**'s *The Art of Looking Sideways*. It's not the kind of book you read from cover to cover. It's one you explore, like a visual playground of thought twists, strange facts, graphic puzzles, and philosophical provocations. **Fletcher** doesn't give answers – he makes you question the questions.

"It's about curiosity. Not about the right answer."
– Alan Fletcher

And that's the point.

Reframing a question is a real game changer. It takes a dead end and turns it into an unexpected door.

It turns **"How do I fix this?"** into **"What would happen if I let it stay broken?"** and **"What should I say?"** into **"What hasn't been said yet?"**.

By flipping the lens – by looking at something sideways – you invite new possibilities to reveal themselves.

The solution doesn't always come from staring harder. Sometimes it comes from softening your focus, tilting your head, and asking the question you didn't think to ask before.

This is also the secret to seeing the world like it's brand new. What if you could look at the ordinary and notice the extraordinary?

That crack in the sidewalk.
The sound of your own footsteps.
The smell of an old book.

Every day we walk past these tiny details without noticing, but they hold entire galaxies of meaning if we slow down and really look at them.
Georgia O'Keeffe, the American modernist painter, once said:

> **"Nobody sees a flower – really – it is so small it takes time – we haven't time – and to see takes time like to have a friend takes time."**

Creativity asks us to take that time.

To zoom in.
To flip our perspective.
To notice what others miss.
Look at things as if you've never seen them before.
Let them surprise you.

We don't see what we see, we see what we want to see. *The Necker Cube* is a simple wire-frame drawing of a cube but when you look at it, something strange happens.

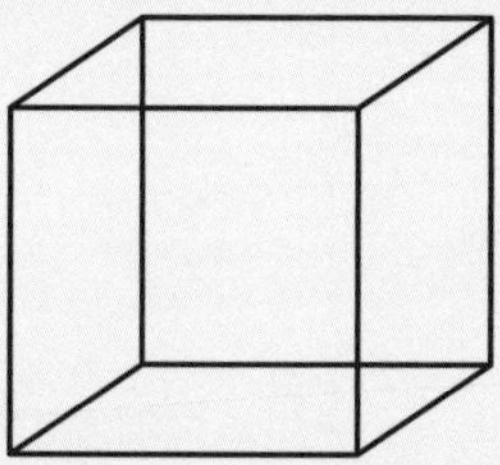

Your brain flips between two different ways of seeing it. Is the front face here? Or there? You can't see both at the same time, but both are possible.

This is the same visual but with a different perception.

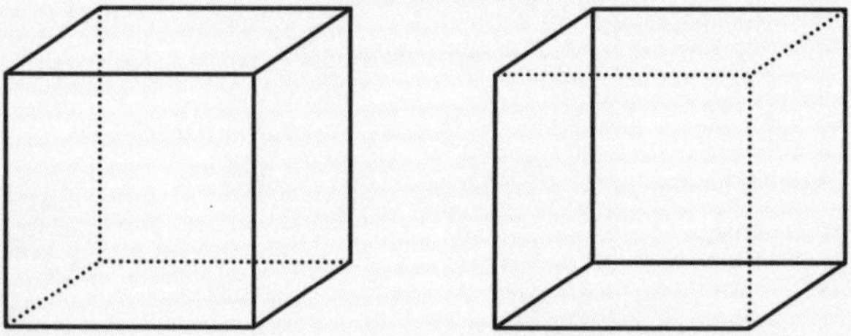

The Necker Cube shows how a small switch in perception can completely change what you experience.

The drawing stays the same. It's your mind that shifts.

Reality is perception, not a reflection of truth.
Now look at the next image.

See the two sets of circles?
Some look like convex bumps.
Others like concave dimples.

But here's the trick – flip the book upside down.

Suddenly, the dimples become bumps,
and the bumps become dimples.
Nothing has changed … except your perspective.

This isn't magic.

It's your brain, doing what it always does: making assumptions. Your visual system is wired to expect light to come from above, like sunlight or ceiling lamps. So when it sees shading, it interprets this as depth based on this built-in model.

Flip the image, and the lighting no longer fits your brain's usual logic – so it rewrites what it 'sees'.

Just like *the Necker Cube*, this illusion reveals how much perception depends on context.

The image hasn't changed. But your interpretation has.

And that's what's at the heart of creative thinking: being willing to look again, from another angle, until something new reveals itself.
Remember this when you feel stuck or when a problem seems flat or obvious.

Maybe it's not the problem that needs to change – maybe it's your angle.

Because reframing isn't about clever tricks or wordplay.

It's a deeper kind of seeing.

It teaches you to approach the world with curiosity rather than certainty.

It reminds you that there's always another way in.
Always a hidden layer waiting to be discovered.

This habit of reframing, twisting, flipping and wondering is what keeps your creativity alive and your mind flexible. It's what helps you step off the beaten path and find inspiration where others don't think to look.
Because ultimately, it's not about being clever.
It's about being willing to see differently.

And that's where new ideas begin.

I AM SURROUNDED BY GENIUS HOPING THAT SOME OF IT WILL RUB OFF ON ME.

Nothing is original.

Steal from anywhere that resonates with inspiration or fuels your imagination. Devour old films, new films, music, books, paintings, photographs, poems, dreams, random conversations, architecture, bridges, street signs, trees, clouds, bodies of water, light and shadows.

Select only things to steal from that speak directly to your soul.

If you do this, your work (and theft) will be authentic.

Jim Jarmusch—American film director

EVERYTHING IS A REMIX

Creativity doesn't exist in a vacuum. Every idea, every piece of art, every new invention is built on what came before it. This isn't just a limitation; it's the nature of the creative process. Everything is a remix.
When you embrace this truth, you free yourself from the pressure to be completely original. You realise that creativity isn't about starting from scratch – it's about gathering inspiration, rethinking what's familiar, and combining elements in surprising ways.

> You have to understand the culture, you have to go to the movies, go to museums every month, read books, listen to music, that's the DNA of creativity.

Consider the music industry. Some of the most iconic songs are reimaginings of earlier tracks, borrowing a melody, a beat, or a riff. In film, countless directors pay homage to their influences, incorporating themes, shots, and styles into their own unique visions. In technology, every breakthrough – smartphones, streaming services, social media platforms – stands on the shoulders of what came before it.

Evan 'Kidd' Bogart did not follow traditional songwriting rules when he wrote **Rihanna**'s *SOS*. At the time he really had no idea what he was doing. The second verse of the song is 80s song titles strung together as sentences because he thought it would be clever. Nobody would think of doing this.

SOS by **RIHANNA**

Take on me, (A-ha)

you know inside you feel it right

Take me on, (A-ha)

I could just die up in your arms tonight (Cutting Crew)

I melt with you, (Modern English)

you got me head over heels (over heels) (Tears for Fears)

Boy, you keep me hanging on, (Kim Wilde)

the way you make me feel (Michael Jackson)

The point here isn't to copy something else.

The point is to transform it.

When you remix something, you're not simply duplicating it; you're giving it new meaning, new context, and new life.

You're showing your perspective on the familiar, revealing connections that others might not have seen.

By accepting that everything is a remix, you unlock a powerful creative mindset. You stop worrying about where ideas come from and start focusing on how to use them.

You take what inspires you, flip it, twist it, and make it your own. And that is how you become part of the long, shared tradition of creativity – a chain of influence and innovation that stretches far beyond any single creator.

"Everything has been thought of before, but the problem is to think of it again." – Johann Wolfgang von Goethe

When Belgian conceptual artist **Kris Martin** rewrote the entirety of **Dostoyevsky**'s *The Idiot*, he didn't try to invent a new story. Instead, he inhabited a classic, replacing the protagonist's name with his own.
In doing so, he made a 19th-century novel deeply personal – no longer just a great work of literature, but also a reflection of his own identity.

This act wasn't about erasure; it was about transformation.

By claiming the text in this way, **Martin** showed how art can evolve when someone fully steps into it.

So let go of the myth of pure originality.
Instead, consider the world around you as your palette.

Everything you see, hear, read, or experience can be remixed into something new, something meaningful, something only you could create.

If you make your bed every morning you will have accomplished the first task of the day. It will give you a small sense of pride, and it will encourage you to do another task and another and another. By the end of the day, that one task completed will have turned into many tasks completed. Making your bed will also reinforce the fact that little things in life matter. If you can't do the little things right, you will never do the big things right. And, if by chance you have a miserable day, you will come home to a bed that is made – that you made – and a made bed gives you encouragement that tomorrow will be better.

If you want to change the world, start off by making your bed.

William McRaven—US Navy four-star admiral

SHOW UP AND BE PRESENT

You shouldn't just wait for inspiration to strike; you have to be there when it does.

I came across this 'make up your bed' quote of **William McRaven** online and it immediately resonated with me. I believe a small thing can be the start of something bigger. So every morning when I get out of bed, I make my bed. Not because I have to, but because I want to. And if one morning I don't – if I walk past my bed and notice that it is unmade – I feel off. I think, I don't want to ruin my day, so I go back and make it. Maybe it is superstition, but it feels good.

Sometimes the smallest gestures can make a big difference.

Some of the world's most renowned creatives knew this, and they swore by the power of routine to maintain that flow state.

When **Haruki Murakami** is in writing mode for a new novel, his days follow a strict, almost meditative rhythm.

He wakes up at 4 am, writes for five to six hours straight, then spends his afternoons running, swimming, reading, and listening to music. He goes to bed at 9 pm, every single day.

By repeating the same pattern over and over, he reaches a deeper, focused state of mind where creativity flows more freely. His discipline isn't about forcing ideas – it's about building a reliable structure where ideas can find him.
The repetition itself becomes the important thing; it's a form of mesmerism.

"I mesmerise myself to reach a deeper state of mind."
– Haruki Murakami

The writer **Maya Angelou** liked to keep her home pretty. But she couldn't work in a pretty surrounding. It was for this reason that, in every town she lived in, whenever she found herself ready to write, she rented a hotel room for a few months. Her routine went something like this:

She rose at 5.30 am, had some coffee by 6 am, left home by 6.30 am, and tried to be at work in the hotel by 7 am. No one was allowed entry into the room. Before she arrived, the hotel staff would have been given instructions only to empty the wastebaskets, and not to change the bedsheets, as she never slept in the room. She also insisted that the room be stripped of any distracting decorations.

So no artwork, no flowers. On the bedside table was a dictionary, a thesaurus, a Bible, books of poetry, a yellow notepad, ballpoint pens, a deck of cards, an ashtray, a glass, and a bottle of sherry.

The simplicity of her set-up and the consistency of her routine helped her channel her thoughts and craft her words.

Even **Ludwig van Beethoven** followed a daily pattern.

Each morning, he counted out exactly sixty coffee beans for his morning brew, then spent the next few hours composing music.

His rigorous approach to both his coffee and his creative process reflects the importance he placed on structure.

What these individuals understood is that routine isn't a limitation – it's a foundation. By showing up at the same time and place every day, they created a dependable space where their creativity could flourish. They didn't wait for the perfect mood or the 'right' moment.

They turned up. They worked.
They made room for inspiration to find them.

When you establish a pattern, you're not just managing your time; you're building trust with yourself. You know that when you show up, you'll start producing. And over time, this reliability creates confidence – confidence that even on days when the ideas feel stuck, your routine will keep you moving forward.

Routine is not just a habit; it's the platform from which you create extraordinary work.

So what about you?

Maybe you need noise. Maybe silence. A specific chair, pen, or drink.

Maybe you don't know your ritual yet – but you can start by looking.

What's one strange little habit that helps you focus?
What's one thing that feels unnecessary but makes you feel more like yourself?

Start there. Let it grow.
Sometimes the weirdest things become the most sacred parts of your creative process.

Think about it.

Creativity is the residue of time wasted.

Albert Einstein—German, Swiss, American physicist

ME WAITING FOR INSPIRATION TO STRIKE, BECAUSE JOHN CLEESE SAID THAT IF YOU JUST SIT AROUND LONG ENOUGH, SOONER OR LATER, AN IDEA WILL POP UP.

IT JUST WILL.
IT'S YOUR REWARD FOR KEEPING CALM AND RELAXING.

DOING NOTHING WORKS

Today most people fill every spare moment with distractions.

Scroll. Swipe. Tap.

And this is killing our creativity.

Dr Nancy Andreasen, a neuroscientist and the author of *The Creating Brain*, studied the brains of highly creative people and identified a surprising and striking pattern in their lives.

They all took time to do nothing.

Einstein would stare out of the window for long stretches of time, letting his mind wander. Mozart composed with astonishing speed, but that speed was likely made possible by long, quiet periods of internal processing – not visible 'doing'.

It might feel like you're doing nothing in these moments – but your brain is actually hard at work.

Doing nothing isn't passive – it's active recombination.

Beneath the surface, a network of regions called the *Default Mode Network (DMN)* lights up. This is your brain's backstage crew, quietly preparing the next act of inspiration while the spotlight is off. The *DMN* is activated when you're not focused on a specific task.

It thrives in the in-between spaces when you're daydreaming, reflecting, thinking about the past or future, or imagining someone else's thoughts. It's the engine of empathy, memory, and mental time travel. Most importantly, it's where creativity begins to simmer.

When you're solving a clear-cut problem, your brain switches to a different mode: focused, logical, linear. But when you loosen your grip and let your attention wander, the *DMN* kicks in. That's why your best ideas often sneak up on you when you least expect them: mid-shampoo, on the toilet, while doodling, or as you're drifting off to sleep.

You're not trying – and that's the point.

The *DMN* connects ideas, stirs memories, and forms new patterns in those quiet moments when you're not looking directly at the problem.
This is why some of the most powerful creative tools are the simplest: rest, reflection, movement, play, and purposeful pauses.

When you stop pushing your brain and let your mind wander, you're not wasting time – you're opening the door to insight.

This isn't just theory. Creatives across several disciplines have noticed it too.

It appears that I have my best ideas just as I wake up. When my mind is not thinking about daily stuff yet and I am still lingering in that twilight zone of wondering.

Paul McCartney wrote *Yellow Submarine* in that twilight zone, as he was drifting off to sleep.

Designer **Massimo Vignelli** explained that he gets his ideas while shaving, which he emphasises, is the reason why he doesn't have a beard.

So remember: sometimes the best way to create is to stop creating – just for a moment – and let your backstage brain take over.

Isn't it wonderful that some of your best works are created while you're 'not working' at all?

Creativity takes courage.

Henri Matisse—French painter

COURAGE OVER CONFIDENCE

Courage is the quiet force that fuels creativity.

It's what moves you to try something new, even when doubt is whispering in your ear. It's what pushes you to share your work before it feels 'ready' or 'perfect'.

While confidence might tell you that you've got it all figured out, courage steps in when you don't – when you're uncertain, vulnerable, or on shaky ground.

In the creative process, courage matters more than confidence.

Confidence is often the result of repeated attempts, built over time through trial, error, and small victories. But courage? Courage is what gets you to take that very first step.

It's what propels you towards the blank page, the unfamiliar tool, or the daring idea. It's what allows you to create even when you're unsure of the outcome.

When you choose courage, you give yourself permission to experiment. You open the door to possibilities you might have otherwise dismissed.

You let yourself fail, learn, and try again.

In that sense, courage isn't about being fearless – it's about taking action despite the fear. It's about showing up, not because you know you'll succeed, but because you're willing to grow.

Courage is also a powerful antidote to the perfectionism that often stifles creativity.

If you wait until you have the right amount of confidence, you may never start. But when you act with courage, you accept that imperfection is part of the process. You embrace the idea that the first draft, the rough sketch, the unfinished prototype are all necessary stepping stones to something extraordinary.

Ultimately, choosing courage over confidence reshapes the creative journey. It shifts the focus from needing to feel ready to simply being willing. It reminds you that the creative path is less about being certain of where you're going, and more about having the bravery to take that next step.

Don't be a cautious creative.

George Lois—American art director

ME AND GEORGE, WHO TOLD ME
"GOD ONLY CREATED A FEW PERFECT SKULLS,
THAT'S WHY MOST PEOPLE HAVE HAIR."

TOO OFTEN, WE HOLD BACK

We erase, edit, doubt, and shrink our boldest ideas
before they even get a chance to live.

Not today.

Today, you're going to create without caution.

No perfect lines.
No safe answers.
No **"Is this good enough?"**.
Just creative courage – loud, weird, and unapologetic.

I met the American art director and design legend **George Lois** twice in his Manhattan apartment, an experience I'll always cherish. He passed away in 2022, but his spirit still resonates in every bold idea I have. His insight, **"asking 'What if?' is the seed to breathtaking creative ideas"**, led me to him and ultimately became the starting point for my previous book, *Creatives on Creativity*. We spoke for hours, and I loved to pick his brain. He reminded me of something essential:

If you want your work to matter, you can't play it safe.

His iconic advice – **"Don't be a cautious creative."** – is more than a catchy line.

It's a challenge. A call to action. A reminder that creativity cannot thrive in the shadow of fear.

Fear is the kryptonite of creativity.

It whispers, **"What if this idea fails?"**, **"What if I look foolish?"**.

Fear urges us to take the safe path, the proven route, the option that guarantees approval. But caution doesn't lead to originality. It leads to the middle of the road, to blandness, to a thousand forgettable ideas that never dared to stand out.

When you choose not to be cautious, you're not choosing recklessness – you're choosing boldness.
You're saying: **"This might not work, but I'll try it anyway."**, **"This might feel uncomfortable, but I'll see where it takes me."**, **"This might not please everyone, but it's worth the risk."**

Creativity flourishes when you step outside of certainty.

It grows in the space where you trust your instincts, take chances, and welcome the possibility of failure as a sign that you're reaching for something new. It's in this zone of bold experimentation that the most memorable, impactful work emerges. So when you feel that urge to hold back, to choose the safe idea, to avoid risk, always remember what **Lois** said:

"You can be creative and you can be cautious, but never be a cautious creative. You will never enter the Pantheon of the Great."

Be brave. Be daring. Be willing to fail gloriously in the pursuit of something extraordinary.

Or as **Rick Rubin** says:

"Failure can be the information you need to get where you're going."

There is no innovation and creativity without failure.

Period.

Brené Brown—American researcher, storyteller

THE BENEFIT OF TAKING CREATIVE RISKS

Let's talk about risk-taking. Because it's one of the most vital, misunderstood ingredients of creativity. We often think of risk as recklessness. But creative risk isn't about being careless.

It's about being honest. Brave.

Willing to step into the unknown without knowing what you'll find. It's about saying something weird, raw, or untested. It's about trying something that might not work, on purpose.

Because that's where the magic lives.

Creativity without risk is just decoration.

It's safe. It's familiar. It might be fine but it won't be new.
And 'new' is where art happens.

'New' is where growth lives.

When you take a creative risk, you leave the safe harbour of what you've done before. You enter a space where there are no guarantees.

Maybe you'll crash.
Maybe you'll find gold.
Maybe both.
Either way, you learn.
You grow.
You become more you.

And yes – sometimes you will fail.

That's not a flaw.
That's the cost of making something real.

SOMETIMES DRESSING UP LIKE A BUNNY
IS JUST WHAT AN IDEA NEEDS.
BUNNIES GALORE!
Fail Better.

Ever tried. Ever failed. No matter. Try again. Fail again. Fail better.

Samuel Beckett—Irish writer

Failure isn't the opposite of creativity – it's part of the success. Each risk you take makes the next one easier.

It sharpens your instincts. It clears out the fear. It teaches you that you can survive a flop and still keep going.

If you want to make something original, something alive, you have to be willing to get it wrong. Over and over. Not because you enjoy falling on your face but because falling is how you learn to fly.

I once gave a talk on failure and decided to walk out on stage dressed as a rabbit. It felt like the perfect metaphor: absurd, unexpected, a little wrong. If people thought it was ridiculous, I was ready to say, **"So what? It's my mistake, let me worry about it. You have your mistakes, I have mine."**
And in the end? That bunny and I ended up giving the same talk in ten countries around the world.

Fear of failure didn't stop the story. It became the story.

Thomas Edison, when asked about his thousands of failed experiments before he invented the light bulb, famously said:

"I have not failed. I've just found 10,000 ways that won't work."

When you fail, you're not broken – you're becoming. You're testing edges. You're gathering wisdom. You're building resilience, clarity, and nerve.

And the most exciting part? Sometimes your worst idea leads to your best one. You try something weird, it flops and in the mess, you notice something brilliant hiding in the corner.

So try. Mess up. Laugh. Adjust. Try again. Let failure be your teacher, not your enemy. Let it point the way forward. Because the ones who grow aren't the ones who avoid failure – they're the ones who use it.

Risk is how your voice speaks louder. It's how your ideas become bolder. It's how good turns into great – and great turns into the unexpected.

So yes, be messy. Be strange. Be unsure.

Your job isn't to impress. It's to explore.

If no one hates it, no one loves it.

ERIK KESSELS SHOWING ME LOVE.

● **Erik Kessels—Dutch artist, designer**

BEYOND FINE

What's the worst thing someone can say about your work?

That it's 'fine'.

Think about it.

'Fine' is comfortable, agreeable, safe. It doesn't ruffle feathers or spark arguments. But nor does it move someone, inspire action, or leave a mark. True creativity, the kind that sticks in people's minds and hearts, often divides opinion.

Some people will love it passionately.
Others will reject it just as strongly. And that's the point.

When the Dutch artist, designer and curator **Erik Kessels** says: **"If no one hates it, no one loves it."**, he's giving us permission to stop chasing universal approval. Because the best work – the work that matters – doesn't aim to please everyone. It doesn't fit neatly into boxes.

It challenges assumptions, pushes boundaries, and creates genuine emotional reactions. In other words, it risks being hated to be truly loved.

So when you make something, ask yourself:

Am I trying to make everyone like it?
Or am I making something that I truly believe in?

The most memorable work isn't safe. It's bold. It's authentic. It's polarising. And that's what makes it unforgettable.

So next time, be bold, be passionate, be true to yourself and dare to be disturbing to others.

Don't be a crowd pleaser.

The thing about a clean sheet of paper is that it still has edges … You can't do real work without edges, without something to leverage, but those edges don't have to be the same edges everyone else uses.

Seth Godin—American entrepreneur

LIMITATIONS

We love the idea of total freedom.

No rules. A blank canvas. Anything is possible.
But when you're faced with too much freedom – endless space, no starting point – it can feel overwhelming, even paralysing. That's because creativity doesn't just need space. It needs edges.

Edges give you something to push against.

They create form, shape, direction. They force you to get clever, to solve, to invent within and around.

The secret isn't to remove all limits.

The secret lies in choosing the right limits that challenge you, excite you, and feel like yours.

The musician **Damien Rice** said:
"A kite needs to be tied down in order to fly. I learned how important restrictions can sometimes be to experience freedom."

You don't need to use the same edges as everyone else.

You get to draw your own boundaries.

You get to define the shape of your own page.

Limitations don't kill creativity – they shape it.

THERE ARE NO SILLY IDEAS,
ONLY UNQUALIFIED ENTHUSIASM.

Amateurs are not afraid to make mistakes or look ridiculous in public. They're in love with what they do.

Austin Kleon—American author

BE AN AMATEUR

Forget mastery. Forget being the best. Forget knowing exactly what you're doing.

The amateur isn't afraid of looking silly.
The amateur doesn't have all the answers – and that's their superpower.
They're fuelled by curiosity, not ego. They ask weird questions, take unexpected paths, and break rules they didn't even know existed.

Being an amateur is one of the most powerful creative mindsets you can have. Why? Because your mind is open. You're playful. You're not weighed down by 'how it's supposed to be'. You're too busy exploring what it could be.
The amateur doesn't wait until they're good enough. They start because something inside them wants to move, to explore, to make. They don't worry about mastery. They worry about showing up.

So stop chasing perfection, start listening instead. Stop trying to perform, start responding – to your curiosity, your instinct, your sense of wonder. Begin again, and again, and again. Not because you know what you're doing, but because the act of doing is the point.

Brandon Stanton wasn't a photographer. He wasn't a journalist. But he started out taking pictures of strangers in New York because he loved it. While collecting these portraits, he began having brief conversations with the people he photographed. After several months he decided to experiment, adding short quotes to the portraits he posted on social media. The result was a bestselling book, *Humans of New York*.
Robert Rodriguez, the creator of *the Spy Kids* franchise and *Sin City*, made his first movie *El Mariachi* with a borrowed camera and a USD 7,000 budget. He didn't wait to be a pro – he just made it work.

Being an amateur means you start now. You make things because you want to, not because someone's paying you or watching. And that freedom? That's where creativity thrives. So be an amateur. Do the thing you have no idea how to do. Start before you're ready. Learn as you go. Follow the fun. Let your curiosity take the lead.
Your courage will catch up.

I prefer drawing to talking.

Drawing is faster and leaves less room for lies.

● Le Corbusier—French architect

SOMETIMES DRAWING TELLS THE TRUTH

There are moments when words feel too heavy.
Too sharp. Too soft. Too complicated.

There are things inside us that don't fit neatly into sentences – feelings, memories, truths we don't fully understand yet.

That's where drawing comes in.

You don't need to be 'good at it'.
You just need to let your hand move.
Let the lines appear.
Let the page say what your voice can't.

Sometimes, when you're overwhelmed – angry, sad, confused – you're so stuck inside the emotion that you can't see clearly.
You're entangled in it.
Drawing can help you get untangled.

Because when you draw what you're feeling, or what you're facing, you take a step back from it – just enough to see it differently.

You make the invisible visible.
You create some space between you and the problem.

When you visualise something on paper – whether it's a work-related issue, a relationship struggle, or a messy tangle of emotions – you step outside of it. You're no longer trapped inside the feeling.

You can walk around it.
Observe it.
Understand it.

Imagine this: you feel crowded by someone in your life. Instead of arguing, you draw how you feel.

You sketch yourself as a plant. You draw another plant nearby, its branches bumping into yours.

When you show them the drawing, they can see it too – clearly, calmly, there's no need for a defence. It might even spark a new conversation.

Drawing isn't just for personal clarity.

It can also be a powerful way of communicating with others – without blame, without big words.

It invites understanding instead of confrontation.

So you'll see that there are drawing exercises in this book that ask you to draw freely.

Not to create art.

Not to be 'good'.

But to see.

Don't think. Just draw.

You might be surprised at what you discover.

DON'T LOOK FOR THE NEXT OPPORTUNITY

This is a trap many of us fall into.

We all suffer from FOMO, the fear of missing out. We think about the next thing, the next moment.

The next idea will be the one that finally ignites our creativity. But in doing so, we overlook the possibility that it is sitting right there, staring us in the face.

Creativity is not a future event. It's not lurking in some distant project or unattainable circumstance.

The opportunity to create is here, now, in whatever you have at hand.

The very thing you're working on – or perhaps avoiding – is the opportunity.

When you stop searching for something better, you can start engaging fully with the present. It is in this instant that ideas come alive, that possibilities open up, and that the work begins to take on a life of its own. By focusing on what's in front of you, you allow yourself to fully explore its potential, uncover its nuances, and create something meaningful.

Don't wait for the next opportunity to feel right or to appear at just the right time. It won't.

This is the opportunity you've been looking for. Embrace it, and let it show you what's possible.

Be a voice, not an echo.

Albert Einstein—German, Swiss, American physicist

I TELL YOU TO LISTEN,
SO YOU CAN LEARN TO IGNORE ME.

DON'T LISTEN TO ADVICE

This book is filled with guidance, ideas, and prompts. But here's the thing: you don't have to take any of it on board. While this may seem contradictory, the truth is, creativity is deeply personal.

No one else's formula or rules will ever fully apply to you. Only you know what feels right in your hands, in your heart, in your process.

When you're constantly looking outside yourself for the 'right way' to do something, you may lose touch with your instincts. You might start creating for approval, for validation, or for someone else's definition of success – rather than for your own.

The real breakthroughs come when you stop trying to match someone else's voice and start trusting your own.

That doesn't mean advice is useless. It can help you see options you hadn't considered or give you a place to start when you're stuck. But ultimately, it's your work.

Your ideas. Your voice.

That's what matters the most. The only real advice you need is the permission to ignore all advice when it no longer serves you.

Trust yourself. Listen to your instincts.

Follow what feels true to you – and the rest will fall into place.

HAVE FUN

At its heart, creativity thrives on joy.

Playfulness isn't just a nice bonus – it's a key ingredient for keeping the spark alive.

When you approach your ideas with a sense of fun, you let go of rigid expectations, ease the pressure, and make room for unexpected brilliance.

Some of your most creative moments happen when you're simply enjoying the process – doodling without a plan, trying a new material just for kicks, or writing a silly story that makes you laugh out loud. Fun takes the edge off perfectionism and reminds you why you started creating in the first place. True originality is fuelled by the return to curiosity, excitement, and wonder.

So give yourself permission to have fun in this book. Make a mess, try something ridiculous, and let play guide you.

Often, the most surprising and wonderful ideas appear when you're not even looking for them. They show up when you're relaxed, when you're laughing, and when you're having a genuinely good time.

LIFE IS TOO SHORT
NOT TO HAVE FUN.

In every person a child is hidden that wants to play.

● Friedrich Nietzsche—German philosopher

Every exercise in this book is an invitation to change how you operate – to move through the world like an artist, a thinker, a question-asker, a creator.

Not because it's your talent.
But because it's your nature.

You don't need to be ready.

You don't need to be good.

You just need to be here.

So let's begin – one small step, one page at a time.

What follows isn't a curriculum.

It's a playground.

Jump in anywhere.

Skip what you don't like.

Return to what resonates.

Trust your path.

This is your space now.

It is time to play now.

YOUR PLAYGROUND MAP

You can jump, skip, wander or sprint.
There is no wrong path.
Just follow your spark.
The only goal is to keep moving.
Keep playing.

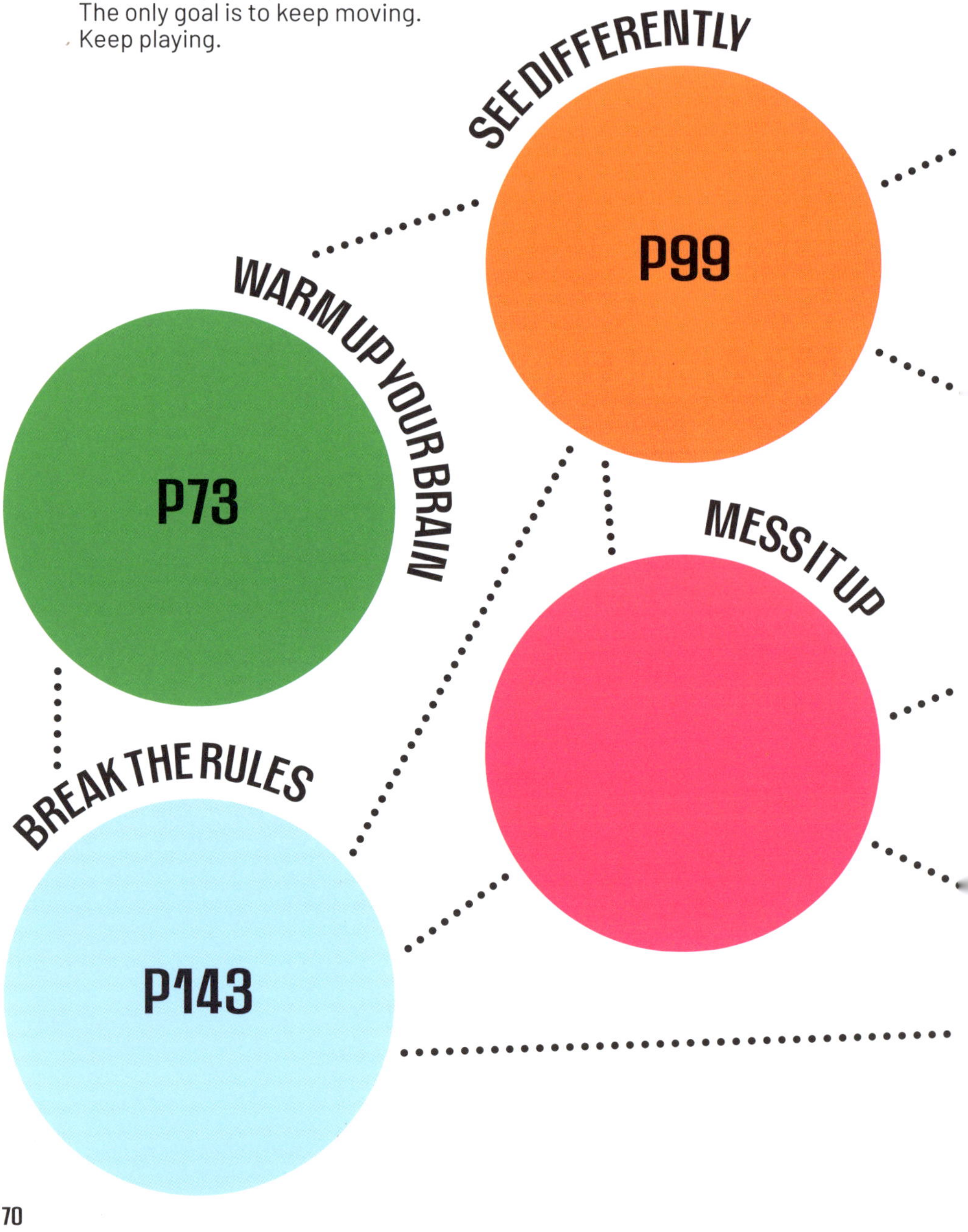

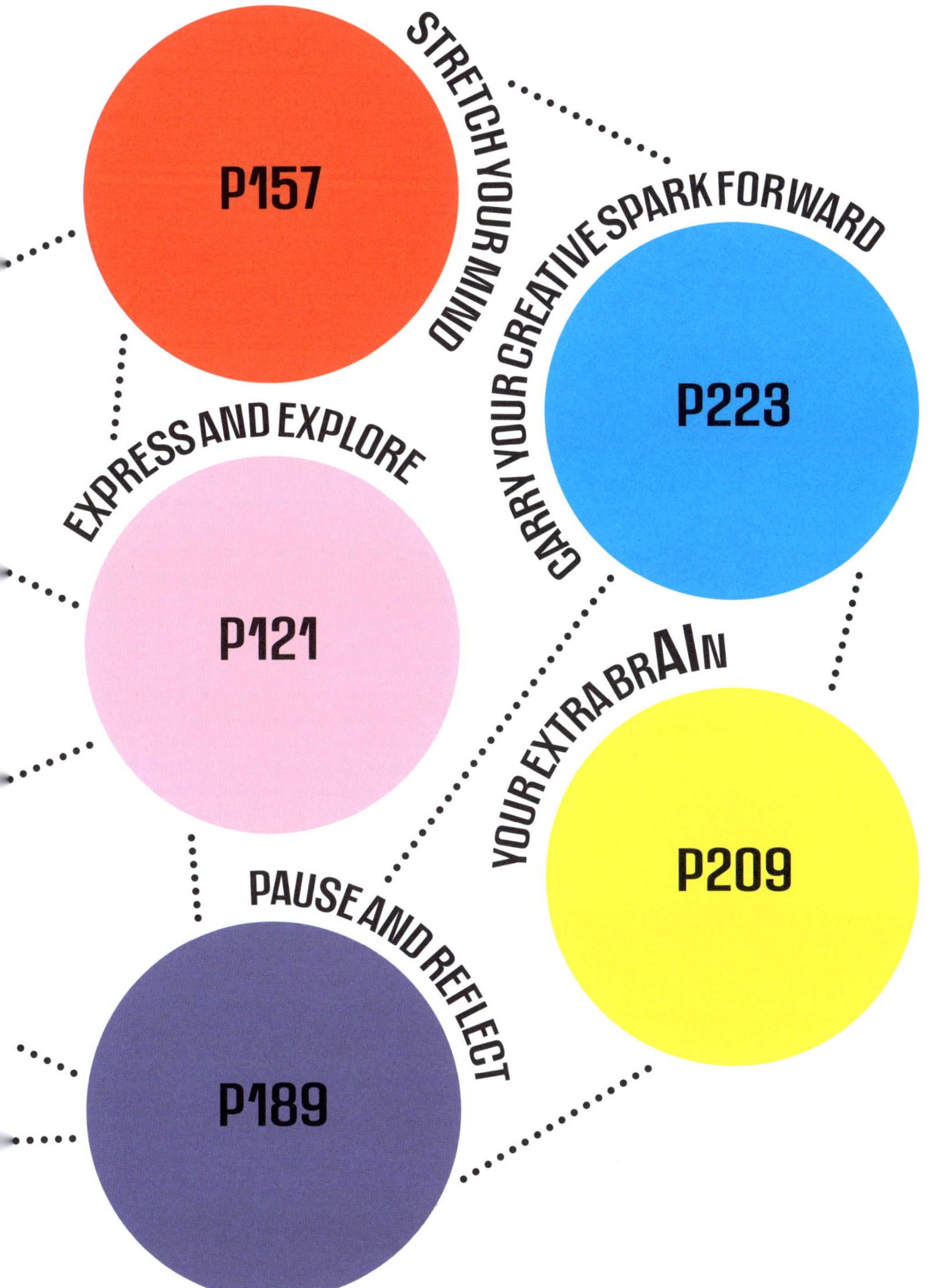
STRETCH YOUR MIND
P157
CARRY YOUR CREATIVE SPARK FORWARD
P223
EXPRESS AND EXPLORE
P121
YOUR EXTRA BRAIN
P209
PAUSE AND REFLECT
P189

WARM UP YOUR BRAIN

FIRE UP YOUR BRAIN

Draw an envelope in one continuous line without lifting your pen, drawing on the same line again or crossing lines.

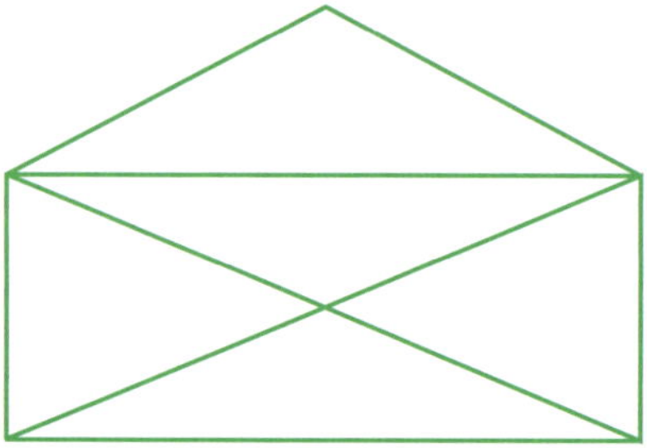

YOUR TIME TO PLAY

SOLUTION P236

CONNECT THE DOTS

Viewing a situation in conventional terms can sometimes create problems that don't actually exist. This is neither a trick nor a test but a demonstration of the human tendency to make assumptions.

HOW TO PLAY

Connect all the dots with four straight lines without lifting your pen or retracing any lines.

Angles are permitted but no zigzags.

YOUR TIME TO PLAY

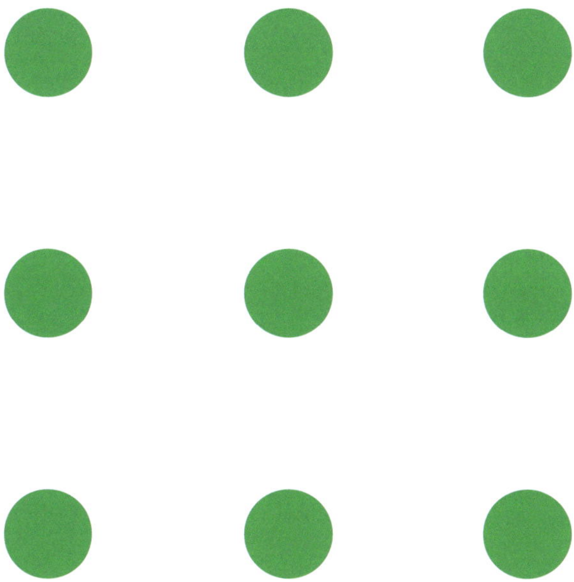

SOLUTION P236

DID YOU KNOW THAT YOU CAN ALSO DO THIS WITH ONE LINE?

If you fold it in such way that the dots are on top of each other so you can connect them with one line.

Again, everything is about how you look at it.

So fold this page and you will see that you can do it with one line.

GO AHEAD, DO IT!

CONNECT AND IMAGINE

HOW TO PLAY

Close your eyes and fill the next page with 27 randomly placed dots.

Now open your eyes and connect the dots without crossing lines.

Take a closer look at the figure that has come to life.

Now try to make a drawing starting from this figure.

You might see a dragon or a plane, give your imagination free rein.

YOUR TIME TO PLAY

The best way to have a good idea

is to have a lot of good ideas.

Linus Pauling—American chemist

LET IT ALL OUT

Creativity doesn't start with answers – it starts with possibilities. A lot of possibilities. A good way to spark many ideas is by tapping into divergent thinking – the part of your brain that throws a party and invites every wild idea it can find.

No filters. No judgement. Just raw, uncut imagination.

When you're in divergent mode, you're not trying to be right – you're trying to be interesting. This is when you should generate as many ideas as possible, even if they seem silly, strange, or totally unworkable. In fact, the weirder the better. Quantity leads to quality – but only if you let your mind wander without fear of being 'wrong'.

There is a story that I love. Maybe you have also heard it. A teacher gives a pottery class a challenge. One half of the class has to make just one perfect pot. The other half? They have to make as many pots as possible. It doesn't matter how good they are, they just have to make as many pots as they can. By the end of the course something surprising happens. The group that focused on quantity didn't just make more pots. They made better ones too. Because while the first group was busy overthinking and planning perfection, the second group was learning by doing – failing, adjusting, improving and stumbling upon great results along the way. The takeaway from this story?

Don't wait for the perfect idea.
Make lots of messy ones. Because quantity is not an obstacle to quality, it leads to it. And even if your first idea is great, don't stop.

David Droga, an Australian advertising executive and founder of the advertising agency Droga5, said:

"For the first years of my advertising career, I probably slept in the agency two or three nights a week. I would literally force myself to write as many ideas as I possibly could. I would do stupid things like take my art pads and fill each page with a hundred squares, all the size of postage stamps. Then I couldn't leave until I'd filled each box with a new concept – even if I loved the first idea – just to explore different creative ways to solve the same problem. As creatives, we are always told to think outside the box. My first objective was to master thinking inside it."

So, let go of logic for a bit. You can organise and analyse later. Right now, your job is to explore.

CIRCLE CIRCUS

A playful, rapid exercise to boost divergent thinking is *The 30 Circle Challenge*.

It is relatively simple to do and takes just a few minutes. The idea behind this exercise is to stop censoring yourself.

It was created by **Bob McKim**. A professor at Stanford University, he was one of the foundational figures behind what became the *Stanford Design Program*, and later, the famous *d.school* (Hasso Plattner Institute of Design at Stanford). He was already interested in creativity, visual thinking, and design processes long before this was trending.

HOW TO PLAY

Grab a pencil.

Set a timer for three minutes.

On the next two pages, you'll find a series of circles.

Your task is to turn as many of these circles as possible into something recognisable: faces, objects, animals, whatever comes to mind.

The goal is quantity, not quality.

Don't overthink it, just keep going!

Often, your first ten ideas are obvious, the next ten stretch your brain, and the last ten ones are where real creativity kicks in.

When you go for quantity, you don't have time to think that your idea is bad, you can edit it later. This is the stage where creativity flourishes.

YOUR TIME TO PLAY

THE GREAT OBJECT MAKEOVER

Are you ready for some creative flexibility?

Take something totally ordinary – and find some completely non-ordinary ways of using it.

Why? Because great ideas often come from the least expected places.

When you train your brain to look beyond the obvious, you get better at making wild connections, flipping problems, and thinking sideways. This isn't just a fun warm-up – it's based on actual creativity research.

In the 1960s, a psychologist called **J.P. Guilford** designed the *Alternative Uses Test* to measure divergent thinking. He would give people a simple object, like a brick, and see how many unusual, creative and uncommon uses they could come up with.

Instead of seeing a brick only as 'something to build with', you might see it as: a doorstop, a weapon, a weight for exercise.

The more ideas – and the more unexpected – the stronger your creative muscle becomes.

This is an ideation classic.

It's weirdly fun, sneakily challenging, and an excellent way to stretch your imagination.

HOW TO PLAY

Pick a simple, common object.
Suggestion:

a glass, paperclip, toothbrush, sock, coffee mug, or shoelace.

Set a timer for three minutes.

List as many alternative uses as you can.

Try to be fast, playful, and a little ridiculous.

Don't judge the ideas – just write them down.

YOUR TIME TO PLAY

PICK YOUR OBJECT

ALTERNATIVE USE

THIS SEEMED LIKE A
RIDICULOUSLY GREAT IDEA
AT THE TIME.
AND THE RESULT IS EVEN
BETTER.
I LOVE IT!

PERMISSION TO BE RIDICULOUS

Let's be honest, creativity is much more fun when you stop trying to impress others.

We spend so much time trying to be 'clever', 'deep', or 'original' that we forget one of the most powerful forces behind creativity: playfulness. That goofy, unfiltered, mischievous part of your brain that just wants to see what happens.

Playfulness doesn't care about being perfect. It doesn't worry about failure. It's the part of you that laughs at your own ideas and follows the strange ones just for the joy of it. And often, it's in those weird little tangents that fresh thinking hides.

Think of this as creative recess.
No grades. No rules. Just you and your imagination, running barefoot across the page.

HOW TO PLAY

THE ABSURD INVENTION AGENCY

You are the lead designer at the world's strangest invention agency. Your task? To create solutions to completely ridiculous problems. Ready?

Pick one (or make your own):

a toaster that sings when it's lonely
shoes that get jealous of each other
a lamp that turns off when it senses drama
a spoon that wants to be a fork
a pen that forgets what it's writing halfway through

Describe the invention in detail.

How does it work? What's its personality?

Give it a name, a punchline, and a wildly unnecessary feature.

YOUR TIME TO PLAY

YOUR PICK

DESCRIPTION

NAME

NOT ALL WORDS WHISPER.

WHEN WORDS MAKE NOISE

Some words don't just describe things – they sound like the thing they describe.
This is called onomatopoeia, when language echoes life.

Think of words like buzz, sizzle, pop, or murmur.
The sounds of these words make the meaning come alive in your ears.

Writers and poets use onomatopoeia to create vivid, physical experiences in their readers' minds.
You don't just understand the word – you can feel it.

This exercise invites you to listen closely to the world around you and invent your own sound words. Because sometimes, the best writing doesn't explain – it sings.

HOW TO PLAY

Listen carefully to the sounds around you for a few minutes:
a dog barking, the crunch of shoes on gravel, a radiator humming, rain falling on a window.

Now invent brand new words to capture these sounds.
Don't worry if they sound silly – the stranger, the better!
Examples:
A bird might make a **flibble** sound.
An old chair could go **grrrrrip**.
Heavy rain might **blup** against the window.

YOUR TIME TO PLAY

CREATE YOUR OWN SOUND WORDS

Mess-making is not a failure.

It's an act of liberation.

Keri Smith—Canadian artist, author

MESS IT UP

Rules are everywhere. Some are useful. Others? Not so much.

In creative work, rules can become cages. We follow them out of habit, out of fear, or because we think they make something 'good'. But often, the most exciting ideas happen when we throw the rule book out the window - and make up our own.

This exercise, inspired by the brilliant chaos of **Keri Smith**'s *Wreck This Journal*, is your permission slip to do just that. Throughout this book you will be asked to mess things up.

Tear the page. Poke a hole in the page. Use the 'wrong' tools.
You will end up creating something that would definitely not earn you a gold star in school - but it might spark something much more interesting. There's no right way to do this. That's the whole point.

Creativity isn't about neatness. Some pages are made to be messy.

Rip them.

Wreck them.

Smudge them.

Set yourself free.

So go ahead. Break something. Then make something new.
You may get a little messy. You may laugh out loud.

You may amaze yourself.

MESS IT UP

TAKE A PENCIL,

POKE IT THROUGH THE CIRCLES

AND USE THE HOLES TO DRAW ON

THE NEXT PAGE.

SEE DIFFERENTLY

MASH IT UP AND DRAW IT

Two ordinary things walk into a grid ...
What happens next? You mash them up and draw the madness.

Creativity often happens when two ordinary things collide and turn into something new.

This exercise helps you train that skill – by drawing the connection instead of just thinking it.

HOW TO PLAY

In the grid, there is a different object in each row and column.

Your job is to imagine what happens when two objects 'meet'.

Sketch something that is a combination of the two things in each of the empty boxes.

You don't need to be good at drawing.

Be weird.

Be playful.

Be unexpected.

Scribbles, weird doodles, and strange hybrids are all good.
If the two objects seem impossible to combine, you're in the right zone.

The goal isn't perfect art – it's creative collision.

**If you had a hat and a lamp, you could draw ...
a lampshade shaped like a cowboy hat.**

YOUR TIME TO PLAY

I GAVE IT A TRY ↓

	HAT	BANANA	BROOM
FISH			A BROOMFISH TO SWEEP THE OCEAN 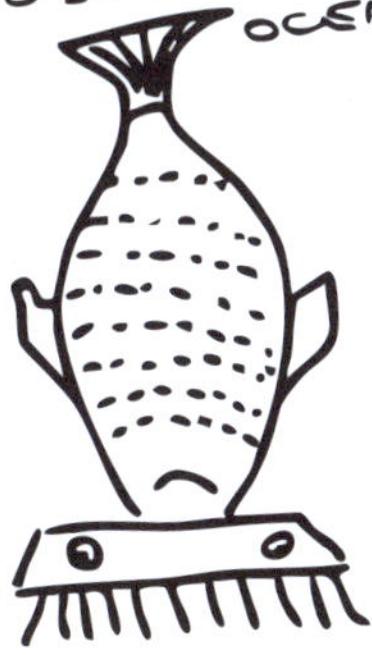
BICYCLE			
BALLOON			

THINK SIDEWAYS

Our mind is built to recognise patterns.

It loves finding shortcuts,
filling gaps, connecting dots.

But creativity doesn't live in the automatic.

It lives in the unexpected.

These puzzles will help you trigger your lateral thinking and solve problems by approaching them from a new and unexpected angle rather than following a straight and logical path.

Stretch your perception and see familiar things in unfamiliar ways.

The idea is not to get the 'right' answer fast.
These puzzles are all about noticing differently.

Some will be obvious.
Some will be trickier.
But that's okay. That's just your brain loosening up.

Take your time. Look sideways. Let the connections surprise you.

YOUR TIME TO PLAY

FIND THE HIDDEN WORD OR SENTENCE

GETTING
GETTING
GETTING
GETTING

STAND
―
I

HE
NOW RE

INVENT YOUR OWN WORD PUZZLE
Use: FORGIVE, WORDS APART

THE MIND SHIFT

d s f b u j w j u z   j o w p m w f t

c s f b l j o h   p v u   p g

f t u b c m j t i f e   q b u u f s o t

j o   p s e f s   u p   m p p l   b u

u i j o h t   j o   b

DIFFERENT

e j g g f s f o u   x b z

SOLUTION P236

TWO SQUARES, ROOM FOR EVERYONE

Sometimes the solution isn't to add more – it's about seeing things differently. Nine figures share a space.

HOW TO PLAY

Draw just two squares to give each figure a room of their own.

That's it. No erasing, no squeezing, no shortcuts.
Just you, a pen, and the gentle challenge of perspective.
This isn't about drawing lines – it's about drawing boundaries with a purpose.

It's also about letting go of assumptions.
Sometimes, the simplest tools are all it takes.
If you see them differently.

YOUR TIME TO PLAY

GIVE A ROOM TO EVERYONE

SOLUTION P236

SQUISH & GO

This isn't just a puzzle – it's a map of decision-making, momentum, and clarity under constraint. There's no undo button. You have to commit.

HOW TO PLAY

THE BUG GAME

You're in a room full of bugs.

Your goal: stomp on each one to squish it and get to the exit.

The rule? After stepping on a bug, you must leave the room and cannot go back in it. Every move counts.

YOUR TIME TO PLAY

FIND THE PATH FORWARD

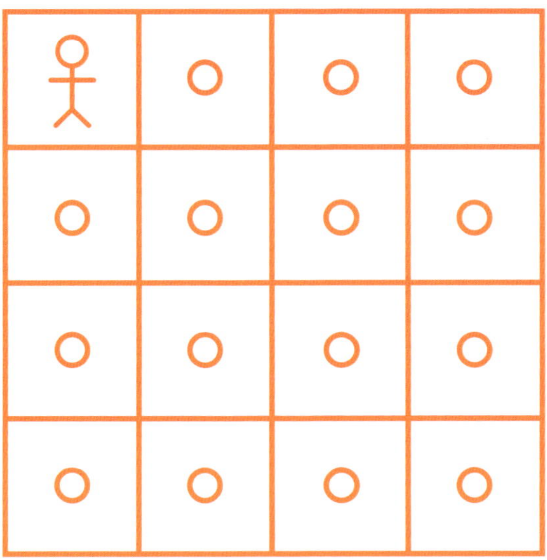

EXIT

SOLUTION P236

THE HIDDEN LINK

Sometimes creativity isn't about inventing something brand new. It's about spotting the surprising thread between things that already exist.

In the late 1950s, psychologists **Sarnoff A. Mednick** and **Martha T. Mednick** developed the *Remote Associates Test (RAT)* to explore this ability. They believed that creativity isn't random – it's about connecting the unlikely. The *RAT* was their way of measuring it, by giving people three words and asking them to find the one word that links them all together.

Ready to give it a go?

HOW TO PLAY

You are given three words.

Your job: to find the hidden word that ties them all together.
Like:

COTTAGE – SWISS – CAKE
(The answer is cheese, of course.)

Some links will come to you immediately. Others will make you pause, rethink, and flip your assumptions upside down.

That's where the good stuff happens.

Take your time.

Trust the weird leaps.

YOUR TIME TO PLAY

1	SQUARE	CARDBOARD	OPEN	
2	DREAM	BREAK	LIGHT	
3	AID	RUBBER	WAGON	
4	FLOWER	FRIEND	SCOUT	
5	HOME	SEA	BED	
6	WISE	WORK	TOWER	
7	TIME	SCHOOL	HOLIDAY	

SOLUTIONS P236

SWITCH YOUR PERSPECTIVE

Changing a story's point of view is like walking into the same room through a different door. The furniture's still there, the light still pours in from the windows, but everything feels a little different. Sometimes, it's the shift we need to see a familiar story with fresh eyes, to uncover hidden angles or notice details we'd overlooked.

In *Notting Hill*, a shy London bookseller named William unexpectedly falls for Anna, a world-famous Hollywood actress, after a chance encounter in his shop. Despite their wildly different worlds, they share a brief, magical connection. But fame, misunderstandings, and insecurity complicate things. This scene takes place after their relationship has unravelled – Anna returns one last time, hoping there might still be a chance. In this exercise, we take the well-known scene from the movie *Notting Hill*, and you have to rewrite it through a new lens. If you want to watch this scene, go to YouTube and type in: *Notting Hill – just a girl*.

INTERIOR BOOKSHOP – DAY
Anna told William she would like to see more of William if he wants to. William can't really express what he feels.
WILLIAM: *... can I just say 'no' to your kind request and leave it at that?*
ANNA: *... Yes, that's fine. Of course. I ... of course ... I'll just ... be going then ... it was nice to see you.*
WILLIAM: *The thing is ...*

He feels he must explain.
WILLIAM: *... with you, I'm in real danger. It seems like a perfect situation, apart from that foul temper of yours – but my relatively inexperienced heart would, I fear, not recover if I was once again ... cast aside, as I would absolutely expect to be. There are too many pictures of you everywhere, too many films. You'd go and I'd be ... well, buggered, basically.*
ANNA: *That really is a real 'no', isn't it?*
WILLIAM: *I live in Notting Hill. You live in Beverly Hills. Everyone in the world knows who you are. My mother has trouble remembering my name.*
ANNA: *Fine. Fine. Good decision, good decision. The fame thing isn't really real, you know. Don't forget – I'm also just a girl. Standing in front of a boy. Asking him to love her.*

Pause. She kisses him on the cheek.
ANNA: *Bye.*
Then turns and leaves.

HOW TO PLAY

Retell the story from the point of view of Martin, the clerk who is behind the wall listening to the conversation.

How does the awkwardness, vulnerability, or tension shift when viewed through someone else's eyes? Capture small details neither William nor Anna would notice. What's lost in emotional immediacy, but gained in atmospheric richness?

YOUR TIME TO PLAY

YOUR SCENE

SOMETIMES I JUST LIKE TO
ADOPT ANOTHER POINT OF VIEW
TO SEE CLEARLY.
FROM ANOTHER POINT OF VIEW.

UPSIDE DOWN THINKING

Sometimes the best way to think differently is to see differently. And you've already done that by just flipping this page.

Your brain is already in creative mode. You took action. You shifted your view.

Now that you've changed your angle, what else might look different?

HOW TO PLAY

Find a place to sit upside down.

Look at the world from a new perspective.

Then write down or draw the things you see and didn't notice before.

YOUR TIME TO PLAY

CHANGE YOUR PERSPECTIVE

Look for what you notice, but no one else sees.

● Rick Rubin—American record producer

SEE WHAT NO ONE ELSE SEES

Not only do you notice things differently when you look at the world upside down.

Sometimes, it's about looking again.

Closer.

Slower.

With more intention.

We live in a world that rushes past itself. But creativity asks us to pause and to zoom in, to really see what's already there.

And the secret is: What you notice is what makes your world original. What do you see when you really look?

HOW TO PLAY

Choose a simple object, place, or moment around you – something ordinary.

It could be:

a coffee cup
your shoes
a window
a quiet street
the inside of your refrigerator

Now … look closer.

Your mission is to find and describe five details that you would normally overlook.

These could include:

tiny scratches
faint reflections
hidden colours
smells, sounds, or textures you barely notice

Write about one detail and tell the story behind it.

YOUR TIME TO PLAY

YOUR OBJECT

WHAT DID YOU NOTICE

1

2

3

4

5

YOUR STORY

HIDDEN IN PLAIN SIGHT

There's a kind of magic in the things that only you notice.

Noticing is where creativity begins.

It's in the shape of a shadow.

Most people walk right past it.

But not you.

You're the kind who notices.

A detail-catcher.
A quiet observer.
A finder of invisible threads.

So is **Vincent Bal** (*@vincent_bal*).

One ordinary morning in May 2016, he noticed something strange: the shadow of his teacup looked like an elephant.

Instead of ignoring it, he grabbed a pen and added an ear, a trunk and a whole new way of seeing.

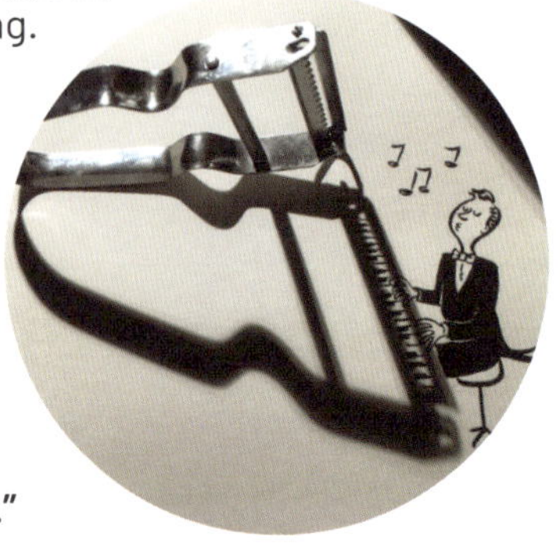

That moment sparked *Shadowology*, his playful art project that turns everyday shadows into delightful drawings. What began as a doodle became a global phenomenon – with a huge following online and exhibitions around the world. It all started by looking differently at what was already there.

Vincent once said, **"I see faces everywhere."** Not as a metaphor but literally. On chairs, on streetsigns and on walls.

Where most of us see nothing, he sees a nose, a grin, a little character waiting to be brought to life. Once you start noticing like that, it's hard to stop.

Your brain starts making connections.

Shapes become stories.

YOUR TIME TO PLAY

On this page, you'll find a real-life photo.
It might seem ordinary at first. But look closer. Is there a figure hiding in the texture? A face in the shadow? A creature peeking through?

GRAB A PEN. START DRAWING. COMPLETE WHAT'S ALREADY THERE.
Let the image surprise you – and show you what only you can see.

SEE WHAT **VINCENT BAL** SEES ON P236

MESS IT UP

SPILL SOME COFFEE
ON THESE PAGES.

YES, REALLY!

NOW TURN THE STAIN
INTO ART.

EXPRESS AND EXPLORE

MORNING PAGES

Clear the noise, open the flow.

Before the day rushes in – before emails, headlines, and to-do lists – there's a quiet space.

Morning Pages are your way into that space.

This exercise is inspired by **Julia Cameron**'s *The Artist's Way*. It's a creative path that encourages daily writing as a tool for unlocking creativity.

It doesn't have to be beautiful.

It doesn't have to make sense.

It doesn't even have to be interesting.

You're just clearing the clutter. Complaints. Weird dreams. Strange ideas. Big feelings.

HOW TO PLAY

Write without editing, without judging, without stopping.

The goal isn't to create something perfect. The goal is to create space, so your real creativity has space to stretch.

Try it: grab a pen first thing in the morning when you wake up. Fill three pages, fast and loose.

Don't reread. Don't fix. Just let it flow.

Even on days when you feel stuck or silly, Morning Pages work quietly behind the scenes.

They clear the fog, reduce the noise, and help your truest ideas rise to the surface.

No rules. Just you, a page, and whatever shows up.

YOUR TIME TO PLAY

START YOUR FIRST MORNING PAGE HERE USING THIS PROMPT
(If you like what you see, continue the exercise daily in another notebook, always taking care to fill three pages.)

Today I want to write because ...

THE FIVE SENSES PLAYGROUND

Create a moment you can feel.

Creativity isn't just about ideas – it's about senses.

The texture of a wall.

The smell of rain on a hot pavement.

The scratchy sound of a record spinning.

The soft colour of gold during the magic hour.

HOW TO PLAY

In this exercise, you'll step into a moment – not by explaining what happened, but by immersing yourself in how it felt.

You'll sketch a scene drawing on all five senses, building a world your body can remember.

Real or imagined.

Big or small.

Simple or wild.

It doesn't matter – as long as you can smell it, hear it, touch it, taste it, see it.

Let your senses lead the way.

Let the memory – or the dream – come alive.

YOUR TIME TO PLAY

Think of a strong memory (real or unreal).
Now instead of writing about what happened, describe the visuals, sounds, smells, textures, and colours you observed. Engage all five senses.

YOUR MEMORY

1 **WHAT DID YOU SEE?** Colours, shapes, light, shadows, movement?

2 **WHAT DID YOU HEAR?** Voices, background noise, silence, music, rhythm?

3 **WHAT DID YOU SMELL?** Fresh air, food, nature, smoke, perfume?

4 **WHAT DID YOU FEEL (TOUCH)?** Textures, temperature, sensations?

5 **WHAT DID YOU TASTE?** Flavours, aftertastes, imaginary tastes?

SHAPE YOUR WORDS

The Korean designer **Ji Lee** (*@wordasimage*) grew up in Brazil and now lives in New York. He believes that ideas alone aren't enough; action is what brings creativity to life.

This inspired him to create calligrams, arranging the letters of a word so that they visually express the word's meaning.

The challenge is to use nothing but the word itself – its letters, its shapes – to visualise its meaning. It's not always easy, but **Lee** says the moment you 'crack' a word and bring it to life is pure magic.

His project *Word as Image* has been featured in leading publications and has inspired creatives around the world.

YOUR TIME TO PLAY

Use: EXIT – TSUNAMI – PARALLEL – MOON – GRAVITY

SEE WHAT **JI LEE** SEES ON P236

Yesterday
an idea is
mine,
today it is
yours,
and tomorrow
it belongs
to the
whole world.

Konstantin Stanislavsky—Russian actor

REMIX YOUR IDEA

Every idea has more than one life.

A single spark of inspiration can become a poem, a short story, a photograph, or a conversation. It all depends on how you decide to shape it.

This exercise is about stretching one idea across multiple forms.

It builds creative range, encourages experimentation, and shows you how flexible your imagination really is.

HOW TO PLAY

Take a thought, a sentence, or a scene and express it in three completely different ways.

Choose a thought or sentence:

She didn't say goodbye.
We buried it under an old tree.
The phone kept ringing.
We laughed so hard tears rolled out of our eyes.

YOUR TIME TO PLAY

CHOOSE YOUR IDEA

WRITE A NEWSPAPER HEADLINE ABOUT IT

WRITE A POEM ABOUT IT

WRITE A CONVERSATION ABOUT IT

MAKE A THOUGHT BUBBLE

What's floating through your mind right now?

A random idea?

A secret dream?

A to-do list and a dinosaur riding a skateboard?

HOW TO PLAY

Use the thought bubble to dump whatever's on your mind - serious, silly, strange, or surprising. Don't overthink it.

Let your brain speak in its own voice.

Draw, write, doodle, collage – there are no rules here.

If you're stuck:

What's an idea you've been too shy to share?
What invention do you wish existed?
What does your 'creative voice' want to say today?
What would you say if no one could judge you?

YOUR TIME TO PLAY

CONNECT THE UNCONNECTABLE

Creativity often begins in the gaps, between things that don't seem to belong together. New ideas are born when unrelated pieces suddenly click, forming something unexpected, strange, or strangely perfect. This is how metaphors work. This is how inventions happen. It's also how humour, poetry, and innovation are built: by combining things in ways that surprise us.

Our brains love to stay in familiar territory. But when we reach across categories – when we force ourselves to connect things that don't naturally go together – we train our minds to see possibilities that others miss.

That's the sweet spot of creative thinking: not just having ideas but connecting them.

In this next exercise, you won't be inventing ideas from scratch – you'll be making surprising connections between words that just happen to pop up.

Let randomness lead the way.
Let your imagination do the stitching.

Let's see what happens when you make something from the in-between.

HOW TO PLAY

Your task is to build a story out of something random.

Go to *randomwordgenerator.com*

Type in the box 'number of words': **3**, 'first letter': **A** (or any other letter you choose).

Click the button 'Generate Random Words'.

Write a short story, scene, poem, or comic that uses all three words in one way or another.

Your words may not seem connected. That's the point. The fun is in forcing the connections, bending the logic, and stretching your brain.

YOUR TIME TO PLAY

YOUR WORDS

YOUR STORY

THE SIX-WORD STORY CHALLENGE

The American writer **Joan Didion** famously remarked that she taught herself to type by typing out sentences of **Ernest Hemingway** over and over to see how they worked. What she took away from this was that his lean, deceptively simple sentences concealed layers of meaning and emotion beneath the surface.

So, can you tell a complete story in just six words? It may sound impossible – but with the right words, even six words can convey emotion, a plot, and imagination.

This idea was made famous by this six-word story by **Ernest Hemingway**: **"For sale: baby shoes, never worn."** In just six words, it sparks questions, emotions, and a whole world of interpretation.

HOW TO PLAY

Try writing your own six-word story.
It can be funny, sad, mysterious, or totally surreal.
Think of a defining moment – love, loss, adventure, change.
Use implication: what's left unsaid can be just as powerful.
Play with tone – serious, poetic, absurd, or ironic.

YOUR TIME TO PLAY

YOUR SIX-WORD STORY (you can write several)

I write because I don't know what I think until I read what I say.

Flannery O'Connor—writer

IT ALL BEGINS WITH A SPARK

You don't have to know what you're going to say before you start writing. In fact, some of the best ideas only reveal themselves after you begin.

That's where creative writing prompts come in.

They give you a direction – but not a map.
You get to decide where things go.

Natalie Goldberg's book *Writing Down the Bones* reminds us to just start. One suggestion she makes is to take ten minutes and write about a meal you love.
She says, **"Write about the food you love most. Be specific. Give us the details. Where did you eat it, who were you with, what season was it in?"**

Another great example is *642 Stories to Write* by the **San Francisco Writers Grotto**, edited by **Jason Roberts**.
It's packed with strange, funny, moving prompts that are built to get those ideas flowing.

No pressure.

Just play.

HOW TO PLAY

You don't have to write something 'good'. You just have to write something real – or weird. Or totally made up starting from a given prompt.

Prompts work because they do two important things at once: they eliminate the pressure of a blank page, and they invite you into something unexpected. Whether it's a mood, a memory, a question, or a wild scenario – you don't have to think it all up from scratch. You just follow the thread.

This is writing as exploration.

Writing as play.

Writing as discovery.

YOUR TIME TO PLAY

Choose one of these four sentences to start your story and get your creativity flowing:

I almost didn't open the door, but ...
Your life changes when you're unable to speak above a whisper ...
You never told your mother ...
The first time I saw her ...

YOUR STORY

MESS IT UP

CRUMPLE THE NEXT PAGE.

SMOOTH IT BACK OUT.

DRAW ON THE WRINKLES.

BREAK THE RULES

THE WORST IDEA EVER (ON PURPOSE)

Here's a secret: trying to come up with 'good' ideas all the time can actually cause creative block.

So let's flip it.

In this exercise, your only job is to create the worst, most ridiculous, most unusable idea you possibly can. The kind of idea that would get you kicked out of a meeting. The kind of idea that makes you laugh because it's so bad it loops back around to amazing.

Bad ideas have value. They loosen your grip. They make room for surprise. And sometimes ... they sneakily turn into something brilliant.

HOW TO PLAY

Pick a problem – choose a simple, everyday problem like:

getting out of bed
forgetting your password
spilling coffee
finding a parking spot
awkward small talk

Solve it ... terribly.

Invent the worst possible solution. Make it totally impractical, hilariously expensive, or dangerously absurd. Examples:

a robot that catapults you out of bed into your shower – on random days
a password made of 400 emojis that changes every hour
a car that parallel parks only when no one is watching

Give your bad idea a name, a funny line, and pitch it.

Go all out.

YOUR TIME TO PLAY

YOUR PROBLEM

YOUR SOLUTION

YOUR PITCH

LOOK AWAY AND DRAW

Forget perfection.

In this playful, liberating exercise, you'll loosen your grip, let go of control, and find joy in the messy, surprising process of pure creativity by drawing what you see without looking at the page.

The goal is to turn off your inner perfectionist and let your hand do the work without judgement.

HOW TO PLAY

Grab a pencil and give yourself five minutes.

However, instead of looking at the page while drawing, turn your head away from the page, hold up your hand and look only at your hand while drawing, NOT at the paper.

Your brief is to draw the creases, folds, and spots on your hand rather than your entire hand.

Oh, and you also can't lift your pencil from the page for the entire five minutes.

YOUR TIME TO PLAY

DRAW YOUR HAND

WHEN OCTOPUSES RIDE BICYCLES

Dreams don't care about gravity, plot, or polite conversation. They hand you a scene where you're riding a whale made of toast through a library of fog – like it's completely normal. Surrealism taps into that same magic. It's not about making sense. It's about following strange symbols, curious feelings, and illogical combinations to see what bubbles up.

It's creativity at its most subconscious and strange.

This exercise invites you to draw, write, or imagine something straight out of a dream. Let the weirdness lead you.

HOW TO PLAY

Pick three random words from the list (or make your own):

mirror
octopus
melting
forest
whisper
elevator
bicycle
feather
clock
sand

Combine them into a dream scene.

Draw or describe a surreal scene using your three words. Imagine it's a moment from a dream. Don't explain it – just create it. It can be eerie, funny, peaceful, or chaotic.

Examples:

A forest where clocks grow on trees and whisper your name.
An octopus riding a bicycle through a hallway made of mirrors.

Let the image unfold in your mind like a dream you're trying to remember.

YOUR TIME TO PLAY

WHAT DO YOU SEE?

START AT THE END

Instead of: 'Once upon a time ... '
You start with: ' ... and that's why they were never seen again.'
... and then figure out what led up to that moment.

It's like rewinding a movie or reading a mystery from the solution to the clues. You invent the ending first, then unravel the path that got you there.

This exercise breaks your usual storytelling habits. It forces you to ask: **"What could have caused this?"** (great for problem-solving and idea generation) and above all it's really fun and a bit absurd.

You are not the first person to tell a story backwards. **Edgar Allan Poe**, a master of mystery and the macabre, believed that a powerful story should be built from its ending. In *The Philosophy of Composition*, he explained how he started by choosing the emotional effect he wanted at the end of his poem *The Raven* and only then did he craft the rest of the poem to get to that point.

HOW TO PLAY

Take a work of fiction that you haven't read yet from your bookshelf and start with the last sentence of the book.

Write it down.

Then work your way back towards the beginning.

You can go step by step or in paragraphs – but everything must unfold in reverse.

YOUR TIME TO PLAY

WRITE DOWN THE LAST SENTENCE

Now ask: WHAT HAPPENED JUST BEFORE THAT? AND BEFORE THAT? AND WHY?

CUT IT UP, SHAKE IT UP

In 1920, the poet **Tristan Tzara** shocked the art world with a radical idea: **"If words could mean anything, why not let chance create the poem?"**

The Dadaists believed that randomness could reveal truths that logic could not. They wanted to break free from meaning, from tradition, from seriousness. They made poems by cutting words out of newspapers, throwing them into a bag, and pulling them out one by one. No editing. No correcting.

Just pure, unpredictable poetry.

This exercise invites you to surrender control and let chaos speak. You might be surprised at what your hands - and fate - create.

HOW TO PLAY

Tristan Tzara gives instructions in *To make a Dadaist Poem*:

> **"Take a newspaper.**
> **Take a pair of scissors.**
> **Choose an article as long as you are planning to make your poem.**
> **Cut out the article.**
> **Then cut out each of the words that make up this article and put them in a bag.**
> **Shake it gently.**
> **Then take out the scraps one after the other in the order in which they left the bag.**
> **Copy conscientiously.**
> **The poem will be like you.**
> **And here you are a writer, infinitely original and endowed with a sensibility that is charming though beyond the understanding of the vulgar."**

YOUR TIME TO PLAY

MAKE YOU OWN DADAIST POEM

MESS IT UP

DRAG THIS BOOK ON THIS PAGE THROUGH THE ROOM.

SMUDGE IT.

SCRATCH IT.

SCAR IT.

STRETCH YOUR MIND

I am always doing that which I cannot do, in order that I may learn how to do it.

Pablo Picasso—Spanish painter

FINISH THE PICTURE

In the 1960s, the psychologist **Ellis Paul Torrance** wanted to rethink how we measure intelligence. Instead of testing how quickly people solved problems, he asked a different question: **"How creatively can you think?"**

The result was the *Torrance Test of Creative Thinking*, a simple but powerful exercise where participants were given unfinished images and asked to complete them however they liked. There were no right answers – just more imaginative ones.

Responses were scored higher for unexpected ideas, humour, fantasy, or rich storytelling.
But even more than scoring, the test revealed something else: how wildly different every brain can be when given the same starting point.

And that's the whole point of this exercise.

Let's see where your imagination takes you.

HOW TO PLAY

Look at the simple line drawings on the next page.

Do both of them.

Turn them into something: a character, a machine, a tiny scene, a joke, an emotional moment.

Use whatever comes to mind. There are no wrong answers.
You can draw, write, doodle, or even add a caption.

Just make it yours.

The only rule? Let your imagination do the finishing.

YOUR TIME TO PLAY

Asking

"What if?"

is the seed to breathtaking ideas.

George Lois—American art director

THE 'WHAT IF' CHALLENGE

Every groundbreaking idea begins with a question. Among the most powerful is: **"What if?"** This question doesn't seek immediate answers; instead, it opens doors to imagination, innovation, and transformation.

"What if?" challenges the status quo. It dares us to envision the world not as it is, but as it could be.

By asking **"What if?"**, we allow ourselves to explore possibilities without the constraints of practicality or fear.

Consider the moments when you've felt stuck or uninspired. Introducing **"What if?"** into your thought process can reignite your creative spark:

What if I approached this problem from a completely different angle?

What if I combined two unrelated ideas?

What if I removed a fundamental element of my project?

By embracing the 'what if' mindset, you grant yourself permission to experiment, to fail, and to discover. It's in this space of exploration that truly breathtaking ideas are born.

Unlock bold possibilities with a single, simple question.

Objective: explore new creative horizons by asking 'what if' questions – without worrying about how practical or realistic they are.

HOW TO PLAY

Pick a project or idea:

Choose something you're currently working on – or something you'd like to start. It could be a drawing, a story, a design concept, or even a personal goal.

Write down five **'what if'** questions for your project.
Let them be as wild, surprising, or out-of-the-box as possible.

Examples:

What if this story's main character lived underwater?
What if I used only three colours in this design?
What if I started in the middle of the plot instead of the beginning?

YOUR TIME TO PLAY

YOUR PROJECT

YOUR FIVE 'WHAT IF' QUESTIONS

1

2

3

4

5

PICK ONE QUESTION YOU WANT TO EXPLORE:

Out of the five, choose the one that excites or intrigues you the most.
Ask yourself:

How would it change the project?
What new challenges would it bring?
What unique opportunities or ideas could come from this "What if?"?

EXPLORE YOUR 'WHAT IF' QUESTION

FOLLOW THE WORDS

In the early 1900s, the Swiss psychologist **Carl Jung** developed a simple but powerful tool to explore the human mind: the *Word Association Test*.

He would read out a list of hundred words to his patients. Each time, they had to respond with the very first word that popped into their head – no editing, no filtering, no getting it right. Even if the response was strange, random, embarrassing, or made no obvious sense, honesty was the rule.

Jung believed that these quick, unfiltered leaps between words revealed hidden patterns – memories, emotions, fears – that the logical mind usually tried to cover up.

Don't worry, we're not here to psychoanalyse you! Your secrets are safe.

But the same technique that once uncovered hidden feelings can also unlock hidden creativity.

Word association is a powerful way to stretch your imagination, break past familiar thinking, and discover surprising new paths through your own mind.

So loosen up. Trust your first instincts. And follow wherever the words want to lead you.

HOW TO PLAY

Start with one word – any word. It could be something simple like:

> **blue** (or: fire, tree, memory, thunder, jellyfish ... you choose!)

Then, without stopping or overthinking, write the next word that comes to mind. It can be related by meaning, feeling, sound, colour, or be totally random.

Keep going until you've written thirty words – one after the other, like a chain of thoughts.

Example (starting with 'blue'):

> **blue – sky – cloud – dream – sleep – blanket – hug – safe – door – key – secret ...** (and on and on ...)

YOUR TIME TO PLAY

1
2
3
4
5
6
7
8
9
10
11
12
13
14
15
16
17
18
19
20
21
22
23
24
25
26
27
28
29
30

Use your chain as a launch pad for something more creative.

WRITE A POEM, USING AT LEAST FIVE OF THE WORDS

DROP THE EGO (JUST FOR A BIT)

Back in 1936, the writer and editor **Dorothea Brande** suggested a curious challenge: write or speak without using the words I, me, my, or mine.

Sounds simple – until you try it.

These little words are everywhere. They frame how we describe ourselves, how we relate to others, how we claim thoughts and experiences. Take them away, and suddenly you have to find new ways of communicating.

You have to shift perspective.

Think differently.

Speak differently.

Write with more creativity – and less ego.

HOW TO PLAY

OPTION 1: write a short letter, journal entry, or story without using I, me, my, or mine.

OPTION 2: speak out loud (or with a friend) for five minutes without using any of these words.

It might feel awkward at first. But that's the point.

Need a starting point? Try one of these:

Describe a place you love – but don't say it's yours.
Write about today from your phone's point of view.
Tell a short story where no one is the main character.
Write a weather report that reflects your mood.
Give advice to someone using the second person (you) or third person (they) only.

YOUR TIME TO PLAY

START YOUR LETTER HERE

Remember: don't use I, me, my, or mine!

WEAR ALL SIX HATS

In a world that often values debate and quick judgments, parallel thinking offers a refreshing alternative.
The *Six Thinking Hats* challenge, originally developed by **Edward de Bono** as a group-based method, encourages participants to focus on the same perspective at the same time. This approach reduces conflict, fosters collaboration, and leads to more comprehensive solutions. For individuals, parallel thinking can be just as transformative. By consciously shifting through different perspectives - facts, emotions, risks, benefits, creativity, and process - individuals can explore problems and ideas more thoroughly.
This structured method helps to break habitual thinking patterns, encourages creativity, and leads to more balanced and effective decision-making. By adopting parallel thinking, you can gain a clearer, more comprehensive view of any challenge, making it an invaluable tool for unlocking creativity and innovation on your own.

HOW TO PLAY

Define the problem or idea you want to explore.
Use the *Six Thinking Hats* approach.

WHITE HAT (facts): Focus only on the data and information you have. Write down all the relevant facts.
RED HAT (emotions): consider your feelings, gut reactions, and intuitions about the situation.
BLACK HAT (caution): identify potential risks, difficulties, and challenges.
YELLOW HAT (benefits): look for the positive aspects, advantages, and opportunities.
GREEN HAT (creativity): brainstorm new ideas, alternatives, and possibilities.
BLUE HAT (process): step back and reflect on the thinking process itself, making sure you've covered all perspectives.

Write down your thoughts under each hat, one at a time. This helps you gain a comprehensive view of the problem or idea from multiple angles.

Combine the insights from each hat to form a well-rounded understanding and develop a more balanced solution or plan. This structured approach can help you break out of habitual thinking patterns and explore your ideas more effectively on your own.

YOUR TIME TO PLAY

START BY DEFINING YOUR PROBLEM

WRITE DOWN YOUR THOUGHT

Use the *Six Thinking Hats* approach:

WHITE HAT

RED HAT

BLACK HAT

YELLOW HAT

GREEN HAT

BLUE HAT

MAKE IT YOURS

Creativity isn't always about inventing from scratch.

Sometimes it's about taking what already exists and twisting it into something new. It's about borrowing, bending and reshaping until your output has your voice, your fingerprints, your point of view.

Artists, musicians and writers have always borrowed fragments of the world around them, remixing them into fresh stories, songs and images.

The French filmmaker **Jean-Luc Godard** said:
"It's not where you take things from – it's where you take them to."

Now it's your turn.

You are not copying. You are not erasing. You are building something new from something old.

HOW TO PLAY

Choose a source.
Pick something simple and familiar:

a famous poem or quote you love
a children's story
a piece of public domain art or photography
a song lyric or proverb

Rewrite, remix, reclaim.

Ways to transform it:

Swap the perspective. (e.g., rewrite *Little Red Riding Hood* from the wolf's point of view)
Inject your experiences or humour into it.
Rewrite it as a recipe.
Remix it into something new. (turn a quote into a comic, or a photo into a poem)

Give your version a new title that reflects the shift you made.

YOUR TIME TO PLAY

YOUR SOURCE

YOUR REMIX

NEW TITLE

LINK THE UNLIKELY

Your brain loves obvious connections – but real creativity lives in the unexpected ones.
When you force two random words to 'make sense' together, you train your mind to leap across gaps, forge surprising links, and invent fresh ideas out of thin air.

It's a powerful way of loosening rigid thinking, discovering new stories, and sparking unexpected ideas when you're feeling stuck.

The stranger the connection, the better.

Stretch your imagination and see what unlikely links you can uncover.

HOW TO PLAY

Flip to two different random pages in this book.

Pick one random word from each page and write them down.

Now find as many connections as you can between the two words. They could be logical, emotional, visual, metaphorical or completely wild. Think of a story, scene, title or situation that connects them.

Example of words found in this book:
ENVELOPE – ELEVATOR

Example of the connection:
A mail system where envelopes aren't delivered by postmen but by elevators that move up and down inside the walls of your house.

YOUR TIME TO PLAY

PICK YOUR WORDS

YOUR CONNECTION

FIND THE SPACE IN BETWEEN

Stories don't always move in a straight line.

Sometimes you know the start. Sometimes you know the ending. And the real creative magic? It happens in the space between.

This exercise is about building a bridge between two things that don't naturally belong together. It's about creating your own logic, your own story, your own set of rules – by connecting two moments that weren't meant to meet.

It's a playful way of strengthening narrative thinking and practicing the art of invention, without the pressure of starting from scratch.

As **David Lynch** once said: **"Stories hold conflict and contrast, highs and lows, life and death, and the human struggle and all kinds of things."**

But here's the secret: even if you borrow the beginning and the end ... The middle is all yours.

HOW TO PLAY

Grab a book – any unread book that's not this one.

Read the first sentence on the first page.

Then flip to the last page and read the final sentence.

Now: imagine the story that connects those two moments.

Don't worry about the real plot of the book. Invent your own.

Write a short story, scene, summary, or even a list of possible events that could get a character from that beginning to that end.

Be as logical or surreal as you like.

You're the author of the in between.

YOUR TIME TO PLAY

THE FIRST SENTENCE OF YOUR BOOK

THE LAST SENTENCE OF YOUR BOOK

YOUR IN-BETWEEN STORY

Poetry is everywhere; it just needs editing.

James Tate—American poet

REVEAL WHAT IS ALREADY THERE

Sometimes the words you need are already waiting – you just have to uncover them.

Blackout poetry is a form of constraint-based creativity where you create something new from something old. You don't start with a blank page. You start with a page full of text. Your job? To find the hidden message.
This kind of creative limitation is powerful. It helps reduce the pressure to 'be original' and replaces it with something simpler: attention. You start to read more slowly.
You notice what resonates. You respond to what's already there. It's a little bit like sculpting: you remove what's unnecessary so what matters can rise to the surface.
Blackout poetry became widely known through the work of **Austin Kleon**, who took old newspaper pages and blacked out most of the words with a black marker, leaving behind fragments of poetry, wit, and wonder. He called it **"a kind of found art"**, and that's exactly what this is.

"It's not about making great art or being a great writer. It's about having fun and looking at the world around you with fresh eyes." – Austin Kleon

So slow down. Black out. Make meaning from what's already there.

boost
your
creativity
and
unlock
your mind.

HOW TO PLAY

Take a newspaper, take a random article, cut it out and paste it here.

Slowly read the words. Circle or highlight words or phrases that jump out at you.

Find a hidden message, feeling, or story in the text.

Once you've chosen your words, use a black marker or dark pen to black out all the rest.

There are no rules – your poem can be serious, funny, mysterious, or completely abstract.

YOUR TIME TO PLAY

YOUR ARTICLE TO BLACK OUT

LYRICS FROM CHAOS

The cut-up technique was developed by the writer **William Burroughs** and later made famous by the musician **David Bowie**.

Bowie would write a bunch of words, sentences, song ideas, physically cut them up into strips, shuffle them randomly and then rearrange them, looking for surprising connections, images or phrases that sparked something new. He would pick out the combinations that felt right and then build lyrics from there. It was a mix of chance and intuition.

One of the best-known examples is *Moonage Daydream* from **Bowie**'s 1972 album *The Rise and Fall of Ziggy Stardust and the Spiders from Mars*. **Bowie** used the cut-up method to create surreal, vivid lyrics like:

> **I'm an alligator**
> **I'm a mama-papa comin' for you**
> **I'm the space invader**
> **I'll be a rock 'n rollin' bitch for you**
> **Keep your mouth shut**
> **You're squawking like a pink monkey bird**
> **And I'm bustin' up my brains for the words**

Bowie saw the method not just as a way of using random words, but also to tap into the unconscious – a bit like dreams.

HOW TO PLAY

Find something you wrote. Anything will do:

> **a journal entry**
> **random thoughts**
> **a letter**
> **whatever**

Cut the page into strips with one word or sentence per strip.

Shuffle the strips like cards.

Pull out a handful at random and arrange them into a new poem, song, or short text.

Feel free to tweak little things so it flows – **Bowie** often did that too.

YOUR TIME TO PLAY

PASTE YOUR NEW TEXT HERE

THE MISSING LETTER

Your brain loves patterns. It's a master of efficiency – always reaching for the easiest, most familiar route.

While this is great for getting through the day, creativity doesn't live on autopilot. It needs friction.
It needs surprises. It needs the occasional dead end.

That's why it's so important to shake things up on purpose.
To flex your thinking in new directions, even if it feels strange or awkward at first.

The goal isn't perfection – it's discovery.

Mike Byster, the author of *The Power of Forgetting*, believes that anyone can learn to become a creative thinker.
One exercise he says will help you become a faster and more productive thinker is to have a conversation without using the letter 'E'. A bit like **Georges Perec**'s novel *La Disparition*, which was written entirely without using the letter 'E', as was its 1969 translation *A Void*.

In this exercise, you'll challenge your brain by removing a tool it usually depends on: one single letter. It sounds simple, but suddenly you have to find new words, rewrite old phrases, and navigate a familiar language in an unfamiliar way.

Yes, really. No the, me, be, feel. You'll have to think around the usual language. That's the point. It's a playful kind of discomfort – and it's exactly what creative growth feels like.

HOW TO PLAY

Set a timer for five minutes.

Write about something simple – like:
What did you do this morning?

Don't overthink. Don't edit.

Remember you can't use the letter 'E'.

YOUR TIME TO PLAY

This morning I did ...

MESS IT UP

CUT OUT THIS POSTCARD.

WRITE A MESSAGE AND SEND IT TO A LOVED ONE.

(OR TAKE A PICTURE AND TEXT OR EMAIL IT)

POSTCARD

PAUSE

AND
REFLECT

WHAT ARE YOU REALLY ASKING?

When you feel stuck, like everything is a blur, or unsure where to start, try this: Write down the question you're trying to answer. What am I really trying to figure out?

That's it.

Not the answer.

Not the problem.

The question.

It might be: What do I really want to say with this story? How can I make this project more personal? What would this idea look like if I weren't trying to impress anyone? What's funny about this situation? Where/how do I begin?

HOW TO PLAY

Your question doesn't have to be deep. It just has to be yours. Something you're circling around, consciously or not.

Write it down.

Sit with it.

Let it guide you through the next part of your process. Because once you know what you're really asking – your creativity has something to answer.

Then write down any and all potential solutions, no matter how ridiculous or 'wrong' they may seem.

Do this for five minutes as a way to focus, stretch your thinking, and stimulate your subconscious.

YOUR TIME TO PLAY

WHAT IS YOUR QUESTION?

WHAT MIGHT BE THE SOLUTION?

Your mind will answer most questions if you learn to relax and wait for the answer.

William S. Burroughs—American writer

STILLNESS FOR IDEAS

While people often think of creativity as 'making things', meditation is about making space.

It clears the mental clutter, quietens self-doubt, and connects people to their deepest creative voice.

HOW TO PLAY

IN SILENCE

Find a comfortable place to sit or lie down.
You don't need to sit like a monk.
Set a timer for five minutes.
Close your eyes.
Take three slow, deep breaths. Inhale ... exhale ...
Then simply sit in stillness and silence.

If your mind races – that's okay.

Observe your thoughts, then gently return to your breath.
Afterwards, open your eyes and write, draw, or doodle:

Where did your mind drift to?
Which images, words, or feelings rose to the surface?
Did anything unexpected bubble up?

YOUR TIME TO PLAY

YOUR THOUGHTS HERE

You see things; and you say, "Why?". But I dream things that never were; and I say, "Why not?".

George Bernard Shaw—Irish playwright, critic

WHY NOT?

A small question that opens big doors.

We've all asked ourselves questions like:

Should I launch that project?

Should I try that idea?

Should I take that risk?

And more often than not, we follow up with a hundred reasons not to. Too soon. Too risky. Too weird. Too late.

That's a dumb idea.

You can't do that.

What would people think?

We hesitate, overthink, and talk ourselves out of possibilities. This exercise flips that pattern. Instead of asking **"Should I?"** – we ask **"Why not?"** Then we listen to the first honest answer that comes up – before fear, doubt, or logic has a chance to jump in.

Asking **"Why not?"** removes the imaginary gatekeepers. It gives you room to explore, experiment, and act – even if you don't know where it's going yet.

It's a tiny question that reclaims your freedom.

So bring your what ifs, your maybes, your hesitations and answer them with more boldness. Because the truth is: the best ideas often start where someone once asked **"Why not?"**.

HOW TO PLAY

Sometimes the only thing between you and a great idea, goal, or change is ... hesitation. Let's shake that up.

Write down one or two questions – big or small – you've been thinking about. Like:

Should I write a book on creative exercises?

Now under each question write:

Why not?

And immediately – without thinking – write the first answer that comes to mind.

QUESTION:

Should I write a book on creative exercises?

WHY NOT?

People will think the exercises aren't creative.

Then do it again.

And again.

We're going to do this for three rounds to dig deeper each time.

YOUR TIME TO PLAY

ROUND 1

QUESTION

WHY NOT?

ROUND 2

QUESTION

WHY NOT?

ROUND 3

QUESTION

WHY NOT?

NOW WHAT?

So – you answered **"Why not?"**.
Now it's time to turn your **"Why not?"** into action.
You uncovered a hidden wish, a brave idea, a quiet dare.
Now it's time to do something with it.

You don't need to leap off a cliff. You just need to take one step. Turning permission into progress.

This next page isn't about making a perfect plan. It's about taking a step. A small, doable, creative step that transforms that whisper of an idea into something real. Even one tiny move can start to build momentum.

Even a messy beginning is a beginning.
Because **"Why not?"** is a spark.

"Now what?" is the moment you strike the match.

Let's turn curiosity into action.

HOW TO PLAY

Choose one of your **"Why not?"** answers.

QUESTION:
Should I write a book on creative exercises?

WHY NOT?
People will think the exercises aren't creative.

MY SMALL MOVE:
I will show my exercises to some friends of mine and ask for feedback.

What could be your first small move towards this?
Big ideas don't need big starts. They need tiny, doable beginnings. Could you ...

sketch it?
talk to someone about it?
google one thing?
write a note to your future self?
block twenty minutes to try it out?

Now imagine your best possible outcome,
just for a moment.

What possibility might open up?
What might change?
What would it feel like?

MY BEST OUTCOME:

I might be encouraged by their feedback and dream up more exercises and end up writing this book.

YOUR TIME TO PLAY

WRITE YOUR 'WHY NOT' HERE

YOUR FIRST SMALL MOVE

YOUR BEST POSSIBLE OUTCOME

DEAR YOUNGER ME

Have you ever wished you could say something to your younger self?

Here's your chance.

HOW TO PLAY

Think back to an earlier version of you.

It could be:

the daydreaming 8-year-old
the insecure 16-year-old
the overwhelmed 25-year-old,
or just you yesterday

Write that version of yourself a letter.

Say what you needed to hear back then. Offer kindness.

Share what you've learned. Or tell them everything turned out weird and beautiful and is still in progress.

This is about reflection, honesty, and gentle storytelling.

Let the letter be as short or long as it wants to be.

Starters (if you need them):

I know you're worried about ...
You won't believe what we've done since ...
You were braver than you realised.
Here's what I want you to remember ...
Thank you for ...

YOUR TIME TO PLAY

START WRITING A LETTER TO YOUR YOUNGER SELF

Dear younger me,

It may be those who do most, dream most.

Stephen Leacock—Canadian teacher, humorist

SLEEP ON IT: LET YOUR DREAMS DO THE HEAVY LIFTING

Some of the greatest breakthroughs didn't happen at a desk – they happened during sleep.

When **Larry Page** was a student, he dreamt up the idea that led to Google. He grabbed a pen in the middle of the night and the rest is history.

Dreams aren't random. During sleep, your brain reorganises itself, reshuffling memories, forging hidden connections, and lighting up surprising solutions. Studies show REM sleep is especially powerful for creative problem-solving.
In fact, people who 'sleep on it' are 33% more likely to connect distant ideas.

Arianna Huffington suggests using this power intentionally. Before bed, ask yourself: **"What problem do I want to get clarity on?"** or **"Where would I like to get fresh inspiration?"**. Write down the question.

Focus on it gently as you drift off.

In the morning, stay still for a moment before grabbing your phone. Capture any images, feelings, or fragments from your dreams. Even a single word can be a clue. When you listen to the quiet whisperings of your dream world, you tap into creativity that's bigger than your waking mind.

Trust it.

Sleep is not the end of creativity, it's the beginning.

HOW TO PLAY

Write down something you want to solve before you go to sleep.

Sleep on your problem and let your subconscious do the work.

YOUR TIME TO PLAY

WRITE DOWN YOUR PROBLEM (and put this book under your pillow)

When you woke up, what were your ideas?

WRITE YOUR DREAMS AND THOUGHTS DOWN

MESS IT UP

GRAB A MAGAZINE OR NEWSPAPER.

CUT OUT ANYTHING THAT RESONATES WITH YOU.

WORDS.

IMAGES.

COLOURS.

CREATE A COLLAGE OF WHAT INSPIRES YOU RIGHT NOW.

TAPE IT HERE.

YOUR EXTRA

BRAIN

AI is not a threat to creativity – it's a partner.

It handles the boring parts so your imagination can do the wild parts.

Eric Schmidt—American, former CEO Google

MEET YOUR CREATIVE SIDEKICK

AI is here to stay. It's not science fiction anymore – it's part of our notebooks, our screens, and our creative lives. Some people fear it, others worship it, but here's the truth: AI is a tool. A powerful one. Like a pen, a piano, or a paintbrush, it can help you create – but it doesn't create for you.

Use it as a tool, not a crutch.

AI is a mirror, muse, or playful sidekick – something that can spark ideas, remix thoughts, or offer a fresh lens, while the soul of the work stays human.

The magic is in the collaboration between human intuition and machine suggestion.

But let's be honest, even sidekicks come with baggage. AI models use a lot of energy, and their growing presence has an environmental cost. So as you explore its potential, use it intentionally, not endlessly. Like any powerful tool, it's best used with care.

In this chapter, we'll treat AI as a partner.
A weird, curious, and sometimes brilliant sidekick.

You're Batman, it's Robin. You're the chef, it's the spice rack. It won't replace your voice – but it can help you find new ones.

Let's pl**AI**y.

THE AI MISMATCH GAME

Let AI spark something unexpected, then make it truly yours.

HOW TO PLAY

Ask an AI tool (like ChatGPT) to write a story, poem, or product idea (this is called a prompt). Try it:

Write a love poem from a cactus to a refrigerator.
Describe an alien pizza shop that only sells emotions.
Pitch a terrible product to solve loneliness.

Read the result – but don't stop there. Rewrite it your way. Keep the core idea but change the tone. Add weird twists or your own humour. You're the editor now.

Make it sing in your voice.

YOUR TIME TO PLAY

WHAT PROMPT DID YOU GIVE AI?

YOUR STORY

TITLE SPARKS STORY

Usually you write a story – and then you think of a title.
But today we will flip this around. A title is a spark.
Invent the story that could live behind it.
Let the title be your lead. Let your imagination chase it.

HOW TO PLAY

Ask an AI tool:

Suggest three imaginary book titles without a description.

Choose one and then invent the story behind it.

YOUR TIME TO PLAY

AI BOOK TITLES:

1

2

3

YOUR STORY

GUESS THE STORY

What happens when you hear just a few words, but don't know who said them, where these people are, or what's really going on? Your brain leaps into action.

It starts weaving possibilities, building characters, imagining worlds.

In this exercise you will be given a scrap of a conversation with no names, no setting, and no backstory.

Your mission? Write the story.

HOW TO PLAY

Ask an AI tool:

Give me a short conversation between two people, but don't tell me who they are.

Now you decide:

Who are they?
Where are they talking?
Why does this conversation matter?

Create the backstory and the future from a few mysterious lines.

YOUR TIME TO PLAY

AI RESULT

MY STORY

GIVE SILENCE A VOICE

Imagine you're watching two people from a distance.
You can't hear a single word.

Only the flick of a hand, the tilt of a head, the pause before a smile. Something important is happening here, you can feel it. But what?

This exercise invites you to step into that silent conversation. You'll listen with your imagination. Reading the gestures, the pauses, the glances and inventing the words that were never spoken out loud.

Was it a confession? A beginning? A goodbye?
There is no right answer, only the story you see.

HOW TO PLAY

Ask an AI tool:

> **Write a conversation where both people only speak in gestures or pauses.**

This is where you come in.

You interpret what they are really saying.

Rewrite the dialogue using words – or just describe what's happening beneath the surface.

YOUR TIME TO PLAY

THE AI STORY

YOUR STORY

AI can suggest, spark, remix – but only you can dream.

Unknown

AI can help you brainstorm.

It can challenge your patterns.
But it doesn't have your taste, your intuition,
your point of view, or your weird sense of humour.

That's your superpower.

Use AI. Stay human.

That's where the magic happens.

MESS IT UP

WRITE A BAD THOUGHT IN THIS CIRCLE, CUT IT OUT, PUT IT IN YOUR POCKET AND THEN PUT IT IN THE WASHING MACHINE.

DRY IT.

THEN TAPE IT HERE.

CARRY

YOUR CREATIVE SPARK FORWARD

You don't make discoveries when you already know what you are doing.

It is important to be ignorant and stupid so you can make discoveries.

Paula Scher—American designer, art director

PITCH YOUR MAGIC

The work isn't done when the concept is formed; it's only done when others can understand and feel it. Creativity thrives in the mind, but it comes alive in the telling.

When I spoke with art director **Paula Scher** about creativity, she shared something that stuck with me:

> **"Your job as a designer is not just to design but to teach somebody else how to see it. The reason why you are a designer is because you see stuff like that and the reason they're not is because they don't. And they don't, not because they are crazy or stupid, no the designers are the ones that are not normal people. They have to teach what they see."**

A rule so simple, but so powerful, that I now use it almost daily – not just in creative work, but in life.

Creativity isn't just about making – it's showing. Explaining. Translating your vision so others can come along for the ride.

This is your creative challenge: to not just create, but to reveal the thought behind the creation.

No one will see the connections you made, the risks you took, or the meaning behind your choices unless you share them. Explaining your vision isn't about justifying it or defending it – it's about giving your audience a way in. When you can pitch your idea clearly, you build a bridge between what you see and what others can experience.

Imagine yourself explaining your ideas to someone who is not in your field of work, a parent or a friend. If you can make them understand, you will probably make anyone understand.

So when you can explain your thinking and the story behind it, people will feel more connected and your idea has a better chance of spreading.

HOW TO PLAY

Express your creative thinking so that others can 'see' your idea as you see it.

YOUR TIME TO PLAY

PICK SOMETHING YOU'VE RECENTLY CREATED.
It can be a sketch, a short paragraph, or even an unfinished idea.

ASK YOURSELF THREE KEY QUESTIONS:
What's the main idea here? What inspired this piece? What do I hope others feel or understand when they see it?

WRITE A SHORT 'PITCH' OR EXPLANATION.
Imagine you're describing it to a friend who can't see it. Explain how it started, which choices you made, and what you're trying to convey.

REVERSE-ENGINEER YOUR DAY

Creativity isn't just about starting something – it's also about visualising the destination.

In this exercise, you'll begin at the end: by picturing how you want your day to end.

Then, like an engineer working from a blueprint, you'll map the simple steps needed to get there.

It's about building the day you wish for.

HOW TO PLAY

Close your eyes. Imagine the ideal ending to today. Be realistic but allow yourself to dream a little.

Now work backwards. Which small steps can lead you there?

Write them down – one step at a time.

And then?

Take the first step.

You're not just living today; you're designing it.

YOUR TIME TO PLAY

YOUR END OF THE DAY

WHAT STEPS ARE YOU TAKING TO GET THERE?

1

2

3

4

5

6

7

8

9

10

MESS IT UP

GRAB SOME LIPSTICK AND COVER THESE PAGES WITH YOUR KISSES.

THE FIRST KISS IS MINE
NOW LET'S SEE YOURS.

NOW KEEP GOING

You made it to the end.

But creativity doesn't end here.

This book was never a finish line. It's a launch pad.

You can return to these exercises any time.

Reread them.

Remix them.

Break them.

Invent your own.

Make notes in the margins.

Fill entire pages with scribbles.

Skip things.

This book is yours now.

There are no rules.

Only movement.

Only practice.

Only possibilities.

So keep going.

Make things that feel strange, honest, joyful, unfinished.

Try again. Try differently. Surprise yourself.

And if you ever feel stuck – just open this book to any page.

Begin again.

NO IDEA IS FINAL

YOU DON'T NEED THIS BOOK ANYMORE

You have everything you need: your curiosity,
your courage, your imperfect ideas.

This next page is your new playground after the book.

Start something.

Anything.

There are no instructions now.

Only possibilities.

Draw.

Write.

Scribble.

Tear.

Dream.

This is your space.

YOUR NEW PLAYGROUND STARTS HERE

SOLUTIONS

P74:

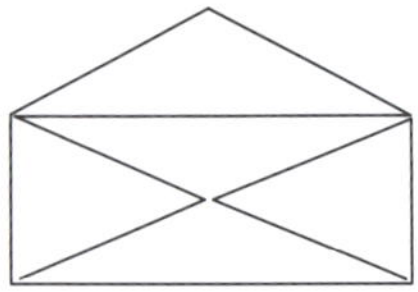

P75:

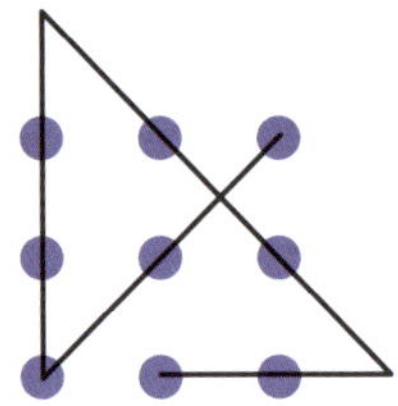

P102: forgetting, I understand, he came out of nowhere;
GIVE GIVE GIVE GIVE, W O R D S

P103: Creativity involves breaking out of established patterns in order to look at things in a different way.

P104:

P105:

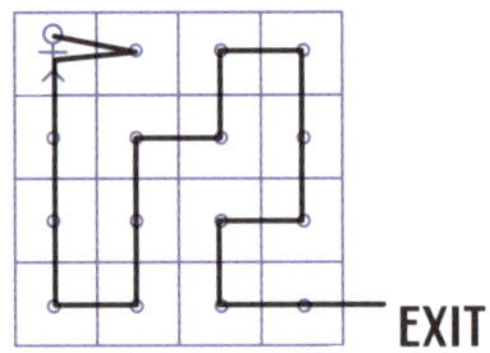

You can return to the room of the person as the rules only state you can't go back to a room where you stepped on a bug.

P107: box, day, band, girl, sick, clock, summer

P117:

P127:

INSPIRATION TO PLAY

It's Not How Good You Are, It's How Good You Want To Be – **Paul Arden**

Whatever You Think, Think the Opposite – **Paul Arden**

Fail Fast, Fail Often – **Ryan Babineaux** and **John Krumbolz**

*Do the F*cking Work* – **Jason Bacher**, **Brian Buirge** and **Jason Richburg**

The Gaze of Orpheus – **Maurice Blanchot**

Creatives on Creativity – **Steve Brouwers**

The Creativity Challenge – **Tanner Christensen**

Atomic Habits – **James Clear**

Lateral Thinking – **Edward de Bono**

COPY COPY COPY – **Mark Earls**

The Art of Looking Sideways – **Alan Fletcher**

Help Your Self! (Dutch version) – **Mieke Gerritzen**

Manage your Day to Day – **Jocelyn K. Glei**

Creative Demons – **Richard Holman**

Six Thinking Hats – **Edward de Bono**

Where Good Ideas Come From – **Steven Johnson**

Creative Confidence – **Tom Kelley** and **David Kelley**

Failed It! – **Erik Kessels**

Newspaper Blackout – **Austin Kleon**

Show your Work – **Austin Kleon**

Steal Like an Artist – **Austin Kleon**

Damn Good Advice – **George Lois**

*The Subtle Art of Not Giving a F*ck* – **Mark Manson**

Hunting the Killer Idea – **Nick Mc Farlane**

Creative Thinker's Exercise Book – **Dorte Nielsen** and **Katrine Granholm**

The Secret of the Highly Creative Thinker – **Dorte Nielsen** and **Sarah Thurber**

Creative Intelligence – **Bruce Nussbaum**

No idea is final – The Talks – **Phaidon**

Turning Pro – **Steven Pressfield**

Don't Read This Book – **Donald Roos**

Don't/Do This Game – **Donald Roos**

The Creative Act – **Rick Rubin**

Wreck This Journal – **Keri Smith**

inGenius: A Crash Course on Creativity – **Tina Seelig**

Start with Why – **Simon Sinek**

Four Ways of Thinking – **David Sumpter**

On Connection – **Kae Tempest**

642 Things to Write About – **San Francisco Writers Grotto**

642 Stories to Write – **San Francisco Writers Grotto**

How to Think More Effectively. A guide to greater productivity, insight and creativity – **The School of Life**

On Failure – **The School of Life**

The Art of Noticing – **Rob Walker**

THANK YOU

First of all, I want to thank **you**, for playing and riding with me.

I would like to thank **Sofie**, my love. For her positivity.
For always believing in me and pushing me to go the extra mile.

Stella, my daughter for turning my words into this beautifully designed book. Better and nicer than I could ever imagine.

Otis, **Henri** and **Matisse**. My sons, for growing up into beautiful young men.

Marc, for asking me to write this book and believing that I could do it.

Dettie, for guiding me through the process of making this book.

Sarah, for her technical knowledge of the art of printing.

Joost, my creative brother and best friend. For always challenging me. He can always turn my crazy ideas into beautiful pictures.

Lien, who together with Sofie spoiled me and took care of me during a vacation so I could focus on writing this book.

Karin, for reading this book and giving me feedback. It is always good to ask people you look up to for their feedback, even when you are afraid of getting it. You will always learn from it.

Sandy, for reviewing the words I wrote and making them sound much better.

Thank you to my parents, **Jef** and **Helga**, for giving me this wonderful life to play in.

BIO

Steve Brouwers is a Belgian creative director, teacher, author, and interviewer, known for his deep exploration of the creative process. With over three decades of experience in the media and advertising industry, he has held prominent roles, including serving as creative director at SBS and Ads & Data.

Brouwers is the author of *Creatives on Creativity*, a book that delves into the minds of 44 creatives from various disciplines, including design, photography, and conceptual art. The book includes interviews that begin with the question **"What is creativity to you?"** and offers insights into the inspiration, processes, and challenges faced by famous artists like **George Lois**, **Paula Scher**, and **Stefan Sagmeister**.

In addition to his work in media and publishing, **Brouwers** is also active as a documentary maker, having created portraits of artists such as **Willy De Sauter** - *Fundamental Painter* and **Gommaar Gilliams** - *A Spark and a Blanket*. He has also written on topics such as blended families, bringing a personal perspective to his writing.

His approach to creativity emphasises the importance of action over perfection, encouraging creatives to embrace their ideas and pursue them with courage and authenticity.

@stevebrouwers
@creativesoncreativity

I TAKE PLAY SERIOUSLY
IT'S HOW I FIND FREEDOM.

Boost Your Creativtity
64 Exercises to Unlock Your Mind Through Play

Research and writing
Steve Brouwers

Text editing
Sandy Logan

Photography
Joost Joossen (P4-5-12-29-43-51-55-64-67-92-110-239)
Kaat Pype (P89)
Steve Brouwers (P37-48)

Graphic design
Stella Brouwers

Postproduction photography
Mieke Geenen – *Pixelxpress*

Artworks, courtesy of the artist
Vincent Bal – *Shadowology* (P116-117-236)
Mr Bingo – *Don't forget to have fun* (P67)
Ji Lee – *Word as Image* (P126-236)

D/2025/12.005/11
ISBN 9789460583889
NUR 640

info@lusterpublishing.com
lusterpublishing.com
@lusterbooks

Printed in Italy

Subscribe to our newsletter for new book alerts and a look behind the scenes: